Pasta

COOKBOOK

Pasta COOKBOOK

Delicious and inspirational recipes for every occasion

Edited by JANE DONOVAN

APPLE

A QUINTET BOOK

Published by Apple Press
Sheridan House
112-116A Western Road
Hove
East Sussex BN3 1DD

Reprinted 1998, 2003
ISBN 1-84092-405-5

This book was designed and produced by
Quintet Publishing Limited
6 Blundell Street
London N7 9BH

Art Director: Clare Reynolds
Designer: John Strange
Project Editor: Clare Hubbard
Editor: Jane Donovan
Illustrator: Shona Cameron

Creative Director: Richard Dewing
Publisher: Oliver Salzmann

Typeset in Great Britain by
Central Southern Typesetters, Eastbourne
Manufactured in China by
Regent Publishing Services Ltd
Printed in China by
Sing Cheong Printing Co. Ltd.

CONTENTS

INTRODUCTION

Pasta – the practical food for today's busy cook – has a long tradition, set in the history of many nations and steeped in the controversy of international culinary claims. Pasta goes so far back in the history of food that it is talked of as one of the first palatable forms of using grain and ways of preserving the milled grain. It is undoubtedly the continued popularity of pasta that has brought about discussion of its origins.

The Italians have to be thanked for making pasta the varied and multi-national product it has become, but whether or not it is fair to say that they invented pasta dough is unclear. From research into writings on the topic, it seems that pasta is a food that has evolved in different corners of the world in parallel, rather than stemming from one particular source.

THE ORIGINS OF PASTA – SOME ANCIENT STORIES OF ART AND TRAVEL

One popular theory is that the explorer Marco Polo discovered pasta on his travels to China during the thirteenth century and took the idea home to Venice. The Chinese were making noodles long before Marco Polo visited their country, but there is also evidence that the Italians were producing an equivalent food. References to pasta-making equipment date back before Marco Polo's travels, and there were recipes for vermicelli and filled pasta in a thirteenth-century publication that also preceded his return from the Orient. The Etruscan art of early Italian civilization includes cooking equipment that could well have been used for making pasta. It is suggested that the first Italian experiments may have been along the lines of a Greek dough.

Apart from these two popularly discussed sources of pasta, Indians and Arabs were also making pasta by (if not before) the thirteenth century, so either could well have introduced the idea to Europe. The names *sev* or *seviyan*, for Indian vermicelli, have evolved from *sevika*, an early name for pasta, meaning thread. Other names for the first pastas indicated that it was long and thread-like, and *spaghetti* is derived from *spago*, meaning string. Later, *macaroni* was to become the generic term for pasta. By the eighteenth century, the same term was used for young men who travelled to Italy with the fashionable intention of improving their cultural outlook, but who, instead, indulged in the pleasures of consuming pasta – dandy macaronis indeed.

A DIFFERENT PLACE, A DIFFERENT FORM

It is interesting to look at the shapes and types of pasta, and similar doughs that have developed in Europe. The Italian-like filled pasta of Poland, for example, was brought to the country as a result of a marriage with Italian royalty, and then there are the robust noodles of Germany. Potato, cheese and flour are all

used as bases for pasta doughs that range from dumpling-like gnocchi to curly spätzle and noodles similar to tagliatelle.

Oriental forms of pasta are distinctly different to these, having a lighter texture. As well as doughs based on wheat flour, rice flour and flour made from mung beans are used to make rice sticks or clear cellophane noodles. Oriental methods used to shape pasta also differ from those of other countries, with noodles being formed by a technique of twirling and stretching the dough. Swinging the dough around rather like a short skipping rope extends it rapidly, and makes exciting entertainment for a hungry audience in restaurants. As the dough flies, it thins and it is folded and swung time and time again to create the long, slim noodles that everyone eagerly awaits.

IDEAL FOR TODAY'S BUSY COOK

One of the first forms of convenience food, pasta still provides an excellent variety of culinary opportunities: there are instant forms, ready meals, quick-cook mixtures and fresh doughs. Thankfully, there are good-quality dried pastas (which have to be boiled for the traditional 10–20 minutes) and these still predominate. With specialist Italian, Oriental and Indian stores in most large towns and cities, the supermarket supply of familiar pasta shapes and noodles can be readily supplemented by the more unusual forms. High-quality fresh pasta is now mass-produced and widely marketed, and inexpensive hand-turned pasta machines are sold in most good cookstores, so it is not difficult to make a batch of noodles at home.

The exciting aspect of pasta is that it can provide whatever you need, be it a really tasty, satisfying supper, a romantic dinner for two, or a stunning dinner party dish. It is all things to all people, from inexpensive novelty shapes for the under-fives to a gourmet topic of conversation for devotees of unusual, enticing ingredients.

The Italians still dominate the world in terms of the quantity of pasta that they produce – 2.203 million tonnes in 1991, with a capacity for an even higher figure of 2.7 million tonnes. Italian pasta finds its way all over the world, but it is still as popular as ever at home, with an average annual consumption of 25 kg/ 55 lb per person in Italy – that is over 450 g/1 lb pasta per person, per week. The rest of us have a way to go before we catch up. Switzerland is leading, at the 9 kg/20 lb per person mark, the USA clocks in at around 8 kg/17½ lb, and Greece manages 7.5 kg/17 lb. The Canadians may be hot on the trail at 6 kg/14 lb, with the United Kingdom having an average consumption of just 2 kg/5 lb per head.

Enough facts and figures, controversy and history, though, and on to the real business of pasta: buying, cooking and eating it. The ever-increasing choice makes pasta cookery a real pleasure, and I hope you will enjoy exploring the diverse world of pasta.

THE WORLD OF PASTA

Italy is by far the most prolific producer of pasta, so it makes sense to begin this book by listing and illustrating the many shapes and styles of pasta *alla Italiana* (refer to the glossary on pages 12–15 to identify these shapes). You will also find information on oriental pasta and the better-known types from other countries in the section on specialist pastas (see pages 16–17). In addition, there is a section on flavoured pastas with tasting notes on pages 18–19.

There are also tips on an equally important group of specialist items; whole wheat, gluten-free, egg-free, and even low-protein pasta; or alternative grain pastas (see pages 16–17).

SELECTING THE RIGHT PASTA FOR THE MEAL

Suggestions for which pasta to serve with a particular sauce are included throughout the recipes. There are some traditional partnerships, with the long thin pastas being served with thin sauces, whilst the chunky pastas and those in shapes to catch juices would be offered with meatier or more substantial mixtures, but there are some unusual combinations to try, too.

Occasionally there are comments about the appearance or the substance of the pasta. This is because they may vary when cooked. You may have come across advice on selecting pasta that suggests that the bright yellow-coloured products are superior to the paler more opaque types. If you extend your view of pasta beyond the narrow confines of the one or two most commonly found Italian sauces by

The basic ingredients for pasta — olive oil, eggs, flour and salt.

shopping, tasting and testing, you will find that this is nonsense. There are many traditional, rather murky looking pale pastas that are more starchy — dare I say it, stodgy — when cooked, but they are ideal for rich, meaty sauces, and not at all inferior to the clearer, more yellow shapes. As a general rule, the only pastas I sometimes felt could be called inferior were some of the really speedy quick-cook types that resembled traditional Italian pasta in shape, but failed miserably in achieving the right texture or flavour.

INGREDIENTS USED TO MAKE PASTA

Pasta is generally made from wheat flour (but see also Specialist Pastas, pages 16–17), usually durum wheat or hard wheat with a high gluten content. Water, eggs, salt and oil or butter may be added. Most dried pastas are made of flour and water, without any egg added, but tagliatelle and pappardelle, amongst others, do contain egg. Read the ingredients list to check.

SOME ITALIAN PASTA TERMS

AL DENTE
'With bite', or pasta that, when cooked, is still a bit firm.

COTTURA
This term indicates the cooking time. For example, 'Cottura: 5–6 minuti' means to cook the pasta for 5–6 minutes.

PASTA ALL'UOVO
This is pasta with egg added.

PASTA ASCIUTTA
This is pasta that is cooked and drained then served with a sauce, as opposed to a stuffed or baked pasta such as cannelloni or lasagne.

PASTA FRESCA
This is fresh pasta that has not been dried.

ILLUSTRATED GLOSSARY OF ITALIAN PASTA

AGNELLOTTI, AGNOLLOTTI OR AGNOLOTTI (1)
Cushions of stuffed pasta, round or semi-circular, attributed to Piedmont region.

AGNOLINI (Not shown)
Small ravioli.

AMORI/AMORINI (2a & b)
Knots. They do not resemble knots, but are hollow spirals that may be ridged.

ANELLINI (Not shown)
Tiny rings, for use in soups.

BAVETTE (Not shown)
Oval pasta.

BIGNI (Not shown)
Local name for spaghetti.

BIGOLI (Not shown)
A type of spaghetti.

BUCATINI (3)
Thick, hollow spaghetti.

CAMPANELLE (4)
Bells. Small cones of pasta with frilly edges. Good for trapping sauce.

CANDELE (5)
Meaning 'candles', the pasta shapes are in fact pipes, about 1–2 cm/½–¾ in in diameter.

CANNELLE (Not shown)
Meaning 'pipes', and including cannellini, cannolicchi, cannelloni and canneroni.

CANNELLONI (Not shown)
Popular pipe shapes, used for stuffing, coating with sauce and baking.

CANNERONI (6)
Larger than canneroncini, these are short pasta tubes.

CANNERONCINI (7)
Short lengths (about 1 cm/½ in) of narrow pipes.

CAPELLINI (8)
Thin hairs. Very fine spaghetti.

CAPELLINI SPEZZIATI (9)
Short broken lengths of capellini.

CAPPELLETTI (10)
Little hats. Small circles of pasta indented in the centre or with a pinched pleat which forms their hat shape. ·

CASARECCIA (11)
Slightly twisted lengths of 'S'-shaped pasta.

CASONSEI (Not shown)
Stuffed rings of pasta from Bergamo.

CICATELLI DI SAN SEVERO (12)
These opaque white curled shaves of pasta are made from wheat flour and water but no egg. They swell significantly on cooking and are recommended for serving with long-cooked meat sauces.

CONCHIGLIE (13 & 15)
Shells. They come in many sizes, from conchigliette for soup to large conchiglioni for stuffing.

CONCHIGLIE RIGATE (14)
Large shells with a ridged texture. Ideal for boiling, draining, stuffing and baking or grilling with a gratiné topping.

CORALLINI (16)
Tiny soup pasta that look like little slices of hollow spaghetti.

DITALI (17)

Meaning 'thimbles', these are short lengths of hollow tube, slightly smaller than the end of your little finger. Good for salads and for a chunkier pasta in soup.

DITALINI (19)

Smaller than ditali both in length and diameter, with proportionally thicker pasta.

FARFALLE (20)

Butterflies. The term 'bows' is also sometimes used for the same pasta shape. Made from thin, flat pasta, these shapes tend to cook quickly for their size. Good for adding to hotpots or layered (moist) dishes in which the pasta is cooked from raw.

FARFALLINI (21)

Wonderful, tiny farfalle, for soups or when small shapes are required. Very decorative.

FETTUCCINE (22a & b)

Flat noodles. This is the alternative Roman name for tagliatelle. Readily available fresh.

FISCHIETTI (18)

Little whistles. Thin macaroni.

FRESINE (23)

Noodles, slightly narrower than tagliatelle and in similar lengths to short spaghetti.

FUSILLI (24)

Spirals, which may be long or short depending on the region of origin. Apparently, they were originally made by wrapping spaghetti around knitting needles, which gives some indication of the size and thickness of the pasta.

FUSILLIER COL BUCO (25)

Long slim spirals (about the same length as short spaghetti).

GENOVESINI (26)

Presumably attributed in origin to Genoa, these are short, diagonally cut lengths of fairly thick tube pasta. Rather like short, plump penne.

GLISTROZZAPRETI (27)

The same basic shape as casareccia, but the cut lengths are curled around into 'C' or 'S' shapes.

GNOCCHETTI SARDI (28)

Small versions of gnocchi, they are ridged, opaque and pale in colour. Good with meaty sauces.

GNOCCHETTO (29)

More yellow in colour than gnocchetti, ridged and semi-tubular in shape. Look more like an average pasta shape than the more gnocchi-like types of dried pasta.

GNOCCHI (30)

Little dumplings. The dried pastas are shaped to resemble gnocchi which are marked with a fork. There are many types of fresh gnocchi.

GOMITI (Not shown)

Hollow corners of pasta, like elbows, lumache (small) or pipes.

GRAMIGNA (Not shown)

Couch grass. Pasta shaped like grass.

I GARGANELLI ROMAGNOLI (3)

Squares of pasta rolled diagonally to make slim rolls with pointed ends.

IS MALLOREDDUS LUNGHI (32)

Like small, pale (creamy white), distinctively ridged gnocchetti but tightly curled.

LASAGNE (Not shown)

Wide strips or squares of pasta. Available fresh or dried.

LASAGNETTE (33)

Small lasagne. The same as malfade, this is a type of wide ribbon noodle with frilly edges.

LE EMILIANE (Not shown)

A name for nests of pappardelle.

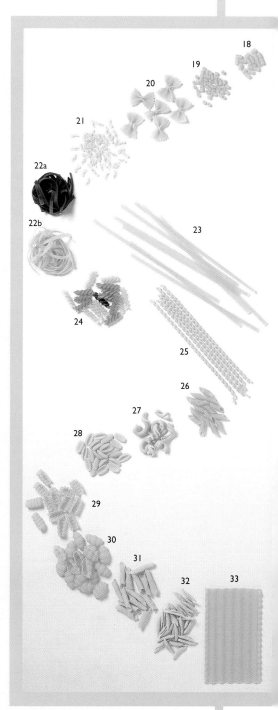

LINGUINE (Not shown)
Little tongues. Narrow noodles or flat spaghetti, readily available fresh.

LUNETTE (Not shown)
A term used on some brands of semi-circular stuffed pasta.

LUMACHE (34a & b)
Snails. Available in different sizes, the large ones are ideal for stuffing. I also found this name attributed to ridged shell shapes – presumably snail shells!

LUMANCHINE (35)
Small snail shapes as above, but not as distinctive in shape. For salads, stuffing vegetables (peppers), or when a reasonably chunky soup is required.

MACARONI OR MACCHERONI (36)
Hollow tubes of pasta, larger than spaghetti. Originally sold in long lengths, wrapped in blue paper packages and still available as such from better delicatessens. Quick-cook, short-cut macaroni and elbow macaroni (another term for elbows or slightly longer right angles) are the most popular and readily available types.

MACCHERONCINI (Not shown)
Very small macaroni.

MACCHERONI RIGATI (Not shown)
Ribbed macaroni.

MAFALDE (37)
Wide, flat pasta noodles with fluted or ruffled edges.

MAFALDINE (Not shown)
Flat noodles with fluted or ruffled edges, narrower than mafalde.

MALFATTINI (Not shown)
Finely chopped.

MALTAGLIATI (Not shown)
Irregular shapes of pasta, cut out with a pastry cutter.

MISTA PASTA (38)
Mixed pasta. Mixed shapes sold together.

MISTO CORTO (39)
Misshapen. A mixture of tubes, spaghetti and broken pieces of similar length.

NIDI (40)
Nests. Small, rounded bundles of tagliatelle or fettuccine, these unravel when cooked. Pasta nests as a base for serving a sauce are created by arranging the cooked pasta in a nest shape on the plate.

OFFELLE (Not shown)
Stuffed pasta of ravioli type from Trieste.

ORECCHIETTE (41)
Little ears. Opaque pasta, paler than usual shapes and slightly thicker than some. With a slightly softer texture when cooked, ideal for rich sauces (vegetable ragoûts or meaty sauces). Look as though they have been formed as the result of someone pressing their thumb into a piece of pasta.

PAGLIA E FIENO (42a & b)
Straw and hay. Green and white linguine or very narrow flat noodles mixed together. Also available as pink and white, flavoured with tomato and plain.

PANSOTTI (Not shown)
Stuffed pasta of Ligurian origins, usually triangular.

PAPPARDELLE (43)
Wide, ribbon egg noodles. Traditionally an accompaniment for rich meat or game sauces, such as hare or meat sauces.

PASTA A RISO (44)
Pasta in the shape of small grains of rice. This cooks quickly and may be used instead of the Greek equivalent, known as orzo or minestra.

PASTINA (Not shown)
Small pasta shapes; soup pasta.

PENNE (45)
Quills. Hollow pasta cut into short lengths, at a slant.

PENNE, MEZZANI (46)
Small penne, slimmer and slightly shorter.

PENNE, MEZZANINE (47)
Yet smaller penne, shorter and slimmer than both the above.

PERCIATELLI (Not shown)
Thick, hollow spaghetti, thicker than bucatini.

PERLINE (Not shown)
Little pearls. Small soup pasta.

QUADRETTI (Not shown)
Small squares of pasta for soup.

RADIATORI (48)
Radiators. Deeply ridged, pale pasta like old-fashioned radiators.

RAVIOLI (Not shown)
Small, stuffed pasta shapes. May be square or round, depending on their region of origin.

RIGATONI (49)
Ridged tubes, like large ridged macaroni. Good with meat sauces and for baked dishes.

RUOTI (50)
Wheels. Cartwheel shapes.

SEDANI (Not shown)
Ridged, curved tubes of macaroni type, resembling celery stalks.

SPAGELLINI (51)
Short, thin pieces of spaghetti.

SPAGHETTI (52)
Long, slim, solid pasta. The majority is now shorter than it used to be, but it is still available in long blue packages.

SPAGHETTINI (Not shown)
The 'ini' at the end of pasta names means 'small', so this pasta is smaller or thinner than spaghetti.

SPIGANARDA (53)
Similar to Pasta a Riso, but consists of longer grains.

STELLINE (54)
Tiny stars. Soup pasta.

TAGLIARINI (Not shown)
Long, ribbon noodles, usually less than 3 mm/⅛ in wide.

TAGLIATELLE (55)
Familiar ribbon noodles. *See also* Fettuccine.

TORCHIETTI (56)
Small torches. Slightly swirled lengths of ridged pasta.

TORTELLINI (57a & b)
Stuffed pasta, formed from squares or circles, filled and folded in half, then pinched together into rings.

TORTIGLIONI (58)
Ridged tubes, like rigatoni, but curved, with the ridges forming a slight spiral on the pasta.

TRENETTE (Not shown)
Finer than linguine or similar to flattened spaghetti.

TUBETTI (59)
Small tubes. Small, short lengths of hollow pasta.

VERMICELLI (Not shown)
Thin worms. The Neapolitan term for spaghetti, which is slightly thicker than the familiar form. However, on an international basis, this is the term ascribed to fine spaghetti.

ZITI (60)
Spinsters or bachelors. Thick macaroni.

ZITONI (61)
Thicker than ziti.

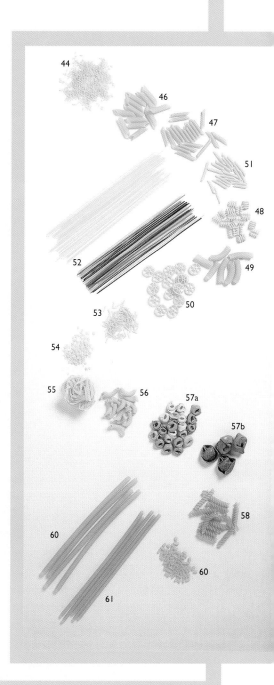

SPECIALIST PASTAS

The familiar wheat flour pastas are also available in organic forms and as whole-wheat types from larger supermarkets as well as delicatessens and health-food stores. However, those who may suffer from an allergic reaction to the protein content of wheat and some other grains will be pleased to know that there is a good choice of wheat-free pasta products. They also provide an exciting range of ingredients for any interested cook. The following is a sample of the range I located, but there are many small stores offering a variety of different products, so see what you can find.

GLOSSARY OF SPECIALITY PASTAS

RICE PASTA

There is a variety of rice pastas, including:

RICE, TOMATO AND BASIL PASTA (1a), VEGETABLE RICE PASTA, RICE (1b) and garlic and parsley rice pasta. They are gluten-free and made without eggs and are available to buy in a number of shapes, refined and stoneground.

The flavour of rice comes through clearly (especially in plain rice pasta) and this makes a pleasant change. Good with thin sauces as the texture is rather stodgy compared to traditional pasta. Take care with the cooking process as undercooking gives the pasta an unpleasant grainy 'bite', whilst overcooking quickly makes it soft. Use the largest available pan for cooking.

LOW-PROTEIN PASTA (2)

Made from blended vegetable starches, including potato and maize. Unusual in appearance for its white colour and a real surprise in terms of texture and flavour. The texture was firm with a good bite (this was a product that suffered very slightly if the timing was not exact, either under or over, when cooking). Apart from its usefulness for those on a special diet, it is an interesting ingredient that looks and tastes good. The lack of salt is noticeable, but this is not a problem if the pasta is tossed with butter or seasoned olive oil before serving.

BARLEY PASTA (3)

A stoneground product produced from barley, it is wheat-free and without eggs. Check the details on the packages you buy, as differences may occur between brands. This has a nutty flavour and a slightly soft texture, with the whole grain adding interest to the texture. Take care not to overcook this pasta.

SPELT PASTA (4)

'Spelt' is a registered trade name for this pasta. Organic and wholegrain, and made from a wheat-related grain. It is not necessarily suitable for those following a gluten-free diet.

The Spelt Elbows that I tried had a smoothness to their texture that is not usually associated with wholemeal pasta.

ORGANIC PASTA (5)

Prepared using only organic ingredients, a wide choice of refined and whole-wheat pastas, as well as products prepared from other grains that are available to buy in the store.

CORN AND VEGETABLE PASTA (6a)

Colourful pasta shapes made from cornmeal with spinach, beetroot, tomato, celery and onion. Attractive and gluten-free, without eggs either. Lighter than stoneground and whole-wheat types, these are a good choice for serving when catering for 'traditionalists' and those who may be avoiding gluten or eggs. The pasta I cooked was good, with excellent texture and a tasty flavour that was not too strong, but justified the pasta being labelled as 'vegetable'. Spinach varieties are always a good test of the quality of a pasta, and I could taste the spinach in these, as well as the onion and other vegetables of the other varieties.

CORN PASTA (6c & d)

Pure corn pasta, made only from maize without any added starch and binders, is gluten-free and made without eggs. Available in a variety of flavours, including:

CORN AND PARSLEY (6b)

Corn, chilli and tomato, and corn and spinach. Shells, spaghetti, twists and rigatoni. I was delighted with the results from the various corn pastas I tried. The texture was good in all cases and it compared very well with Italian

wheat pasta. Also, the flavour was delicate and pleasing and would go well with any pasta sauce. The types I tried were not temperamental in the cooking, so a couple of minutes too little or long did not spoil them.

WHOLE-WHEAT PASTA (7)
There is a wide variety of whole-wheat pasta products available, from supermarkets as well as specialist stores.

RICE AND MILLET PASTA (8)
Stoneground, wholegrain pasta that is wheat- and gluten-free. It is also made without eggs.

KAMUT PASTA (9a & b)
Kamut is a registered trade name for a range of Italian pasta products. Marketed as wholegrain and organic, the information on the package provides promotional information on the ingredients without giving details of exactly what goes into the pasta

product, other than a reference to *Triticum polonicum* after the trade name. *Triticum* is the Latin name for a wild species of grain from which wheat developed (the Latin name of durum wheat is *Triticum durum* for this reason). It should not be eaten by those following a gluten-free diet.

When cooked, the pasta I tried became quite pale. It was firm and *al dente* in texture. Anyone used to eating a high-fibre whole-wheat pasta would probably find the texture too smooth, light, soft or plain, and it cannot be compared directly with whole-wheat pasta in terms of texture. I found it to be similar to white bread with fibre added.

BUCKWHEAT PASTA (Not shown)
Made without wheat flour, this is suitable for those following a gluten-free diet. Note, though, that Japanese soba noodles are also made from buckwheat flour, but are often

combined with wheat flour, so, if you are allergic to wheat, take care when selecting Japanese-style noodles as some oriental labelling suffers badly from translation difficulties.

COOKING NOTE
I found that some of the cooking times suggested by manufacturers of specialist pastas were quite inaccurate. In particular, some of the very short cooking times were too short and the pasta was just not cooked. When using a new product, it is worth checking the pasta at different stages during boiling. Also, you will need a large pan for some specialist pastas as they tend to make the water starchy.

FLAVOURED PASTAS

There is a wide choice of flavoured pasta products and the quality is equally varied,

but then this is true of all food products. The information that follows applies to the dried pastas that I tried.

Some of the flavoured fresh pastas, particularly the less expensive brands, can be rather coarse and raw in taste.

By way of contrast, some of the best fresh pastas really are a treat.

GLOSSARY OF FLAVOURED PASTAS

PORCINI PASTA

Delicious pasta flavoured with dried ceps or porcini. A distinctly flavoured pasta that will stand alone if dressed with a little butter, oil, cream or other very simple sauce. Clever mushroom shapes enhanced the image. Would be terrific in a hearty mushroom soup (it was a shame to drain away their cooking water) or in hotpots and moist stews. The expensive Italian brand I tried really was worth it.

CORN AND SPINACH PASTA

See Speciality Pastas. The combination of corn and spinach was good in flavour and colour. Good spinach colour.

BLACK SQUID

Cuttlefish or squid ink is used to enrich rather than strongly flavour the pasta. Although squid ink pastas do not have a 'fishy' flavour they are tinged with seafood and I would not serve them with a poultry sauce or meat. Best for seafood or vegetable-based sauces.

TOMATO

As for spinach, the quality varies significantly and some pink pasta tastes rather bland.

SMOKED SALMON

The pasta smelled strongly of smoked salmon, but the flavour had diminished markedly after boiling. For the price, I recommend buying regular pasta and spending the price difference on fresh smoked salmon to toss into it.

CORN, TOMATO AND CHILLI

See Corn Pasta in the Glossary of Speciality Pastas. Quite distinctly tasted of chilli, but the tomato does not come through. Good in flavour and texture.

GARLIC AND CHILLI

The Italian brand I tried was good (spaghetti), with a pronounced pep coming from the chilli.

CHIANTI SPECIALITY

Novelty pasta in the shapes of red grapes (beetroot), white grapes (plain) and leaves (spinach). This was very good, and the spinach flavour was the best of all the spinach pastas that I tried. Looks terrific!

BLACK AND WHITE SPAGHETTI

Flavoured with black squid ink and plain. A good combination that makes an elegant base for seafood. A smart option for appearance rather than flavour.

ASPARAGUS

At first taste, a bit "grassy," but better when tossed with melted butter. Serve with a light, creamy, or milk sauce.

FASTA PASTA

There is a wide range of quick-cook pasta, instant noodles and sauced pasta. Here are just a few of them.

BOIL-IN-THE-BAG PASTA
Perforated boiling bags containing slim fusilli (spirals or other shapes) that cook in about 7–8 minutes. Easy to drain, but the texture is not as good as 'proper' pasta.

INSTANT CHINESE NOODLES
These are soaked in freshly boiled water instead of having to be boiled. They are great; especially for supper-in-a-hurry dishes.

INSTANT OR VERY SPEEDY PASTAS
These are usually in cake form, like Chinese dried noodles, and vary considerably in quality and flavour. In general, I find that the more they offer in the way of flavouring, the less like real food they tend to be.

QUICK-COOK PASTAS
Spaghetti in a major Italian range cooks in 3 minutes to give excellent results, but some larger shapes tend to have a slightly slimy texture. Quick-cook macaronis vary; some are ready in 3 minutes, others in 7 minutes. I found the latter to be excellent.

SAUCED DRIED PASTA
There is an ever-increasing and changing range of dehydrated sauce and pasta mixes, rather like flavoured rice mixes. Frankly, with fresh pasta so readily available, I would opt for a bowl of pasta topped with a little oil or butter and some grated cheese.

BLACK OLIVE SPAGHETTI
This is good! A light flavour of black olives that is just sufficient to assert itself. Ideal for tossing with olive oil and garlic and topping with Romano. Would be lost with a strong (meat-type) sauce, milk, or cream. Diced fresh tomatoes or sun-dried tomatoes would go well, especially with fresh basil or parsley.

GARLIC AND TOMATO
The garlic tends to overpower the tomato, so the latter contributes colour rather than flavour.

SPINACH
Qualities vary widely, but expensive types are worth the extra for a good spinach flavour.

CHAMPIGNON
From a French range, the '*pâtes aux oeufs frais aromatisées*' that I tried were flavoured with dried *trompettes de mort* mushrooms. A good flavour, milder than porcini pasta. Serve plain with butter, oil or cream and cheese. Toss with sautéed mushrooms to accentuate the flavour or toss with butter and serve as a base for creamy chicken mixtures or milk-based seafood sauces. Take care not to drown the delicate mushroom flavour.

BASIL
Quality is important when buying herb-flavoured pasta. I tried a French-made brand of tagliatelle that had a good, mild basil flavour. Good tossed with oil or butter as a base for a topping or simply with cheese.

PASTA IN THE DIET

What sort of image does pasta have in your household and when does pasta immediately spring to mind as the ideal ingredient for a meal?

The popular image of pasta is Italian, quick, easy, nutritious, slimming and . . . creative.

Let us pause to take a longer look at some of these ideas.

Does our experience of cooking and eating pasta reinforce or dispel these popular ideas?

I think pasta is a terrific, versatile ingredient; better still, it can be delicious and different to eat in very many ways.

I hope that the following pages expand your repertoire.

The important factor to remember about pasta is that it is not eaten on its own.

Therefore, its true food value in the diet is subject to the accompaniments offered with it or the dishes for which it is an aside. This is very important.

If you have a serious interest in the food value of pasta, then you will appreciate that this varies according to the product.

Apart from the completely separate types of pasta – Chinese, Japanese, Italian – there are regional specialities, foreign interpretations, fast foods and many brands.

The information manufacturers put on their packaging is erratic in the detail it provides, and it is not possible to provide accurate information to cover all pasta types.

However, it is helpful to offer general guidance.

Linguini with Green Peppers and Pesto

PUTTING THE WORD 'DIET' INTO PERSPECTIVE

First, I ought to stress that the word 'diet' is used here in the nutritional sense, that is, to refer to all food that is eaten, regardless of any specific characteristics relating to individuals and specific types of diet. I do not use it to indicate a 'reduced calorie' or 'calorie controlled' diet. Also, this information is based on Italian-type pasta rather than Oriental pasta, such as rice sticks or won ton dough.

A WELL-BALANCED DIET

Advertisements bombard the public with information about 'healthy' foods, but in fact there is no such thing as an unhealthy food. Butter, cream and other high-fat products are all relevant in a balanced diet as long as they are eaten as a *small* proportion of a varied total food intake. On an everyday basis, we should all consume significantly more starch and fresh fruit and vegetables than protein and fat; and we should consume regular and frequent supplies of dietary fibre or non-starch polysaccharides. Variety is probably the most useful key to a well-balanced diet.

PASTA: A USEFUL FOOD FOR SENSIBLE EATING

Pasta is a useful food to include in a well-balanced diet. In itself, it does not have a high fat content, it provides starch for energy, and it may include a small but useful source of protein. Egg pasta can make a valuable contribution of protein to a vegetarian diet where many different sources make up the total intake, unlike a diet based on fish, poultry or meat where concentrated sources of animal protein are eaten regularly.

As pasta is often eaten with substantial salads, it can be a useful food for promoting healthy eating.

There are many excellent sauces and accompaniments that substantiate the image of pasta as a well-balanced, healthy food. However, there is also a distinct tendency to smother pasta with olive oil, butter, cream and cheese, so it is up to us whether we eat it in a healthy or less healthy way.

PASTA FOR ENERGY: A CARBOHYDRATE FOOD

Primarily, pasta is a carbohydrate food, usually based on wheat. Its main contribution to diet is starch. However, depending on the type, as we have seen, the pasta may also make a contribution of protein (not that protein is a nutrient generally lacking in the Western diet). It also provides some minerals and contributes a small amount of certain vitamins.

To put this into context, pasta is similar to potatoes or rice in its role in our diet. Starches should be the main source of energy in the diet (as opposed to sugars and fats). The body breaks down food to obtain energy. Simple sugars are most easily broken down and starch, which does not have a high fibre content, is digested more quickly than foods that contain a significant amount of fibre.

ALL-IMPORTANT FIBRE

Fibre is essential in the diet. White pasta is *not* a valuable source of fibre, but whole-wheat pasta does provide a useful supply of dietary fibre, or non-starch polysaccharides as the experts would like it termed.

PASTA AND FAT: COMPARISONS

Pasta is often promoted as a low-fat food. It does have a low fat content in itself and, when olive oil is used in its manufacture, the greater percentage of the fat it does have may be mono-unsaturated. Potatoes, rice and wheat are also low-fat foods, and they may contain less fat than pasta.

For example, 100 g/4 oz raw macaroni contains about 1.8 grammes fat; a similar weight of raw potato contains 0.2 grammes fat. As 100 g/4 oz raw potato is hardly a representative portion and 100 g/4 oz macaroni is a generous portion, a better comparison is between 100 g/4 oz raw macaroni with 1.8 grammes fat and 300 g/12 oz raw potato with 0.7 grammes fat: the macaroni has more than double the quantity of fat in the potato.

This comparison can be made between egg noodles and various other types of pasta with similar indications. It is also interesting to compare pasta with rice. Rice has a higher fat content than potatoes, but it is lower than pasta.

I am adopting a pedantic approach and splitting hairs simply to put pasta into context, but pasta, potatoes and rice are all carbohydrate-rich foods which have a low fat content. The actual fat content of pasta depends on the ingredients used to make it – it is a product, not produce.

Tagliatelle with Grated Carrot and Spring Onion

PASTA AND CALORIE-CONTROLLED DIETS

Pasta is a useful food to eat when following a reduced-calorie or calorie-controlled diet because it provides reasonable bulk for its calorie content. The same is true of any food that has a high starch and low fat content, such as potatoes and rice.

One of the difficulties of promoting pasta as useful in low-calorie diets and when slimming is in distinguishing the low-calorie dishes with pasta from the others, which are calorific. For example, a hearty bowl of boiled pasta with steamed courgettes, tossed with fresh basil and topped with 2 tablespoons of grated Parmesan cheese, plenty of black pepper and 1 tablespoon of yoghurt is every slimmer's dream meal. However, the simpler alternative of pasta tossed with olive oil and garlic and served with a bowl of Parmesan or Romano to taste will provide a far higher calorie intake, quite out of the realms of the target for a low-calorie meal.

TEN CALORIE-COUNTED TOPPINGS

The calorie counts for the following are a guide for the ingredients given, excluding the pasta. Each idea provides a single serving.

1 Thinly slice 100 g/4 oz young courgette. Steam them over boiling water for 5 minutes, cook them in the microwave for about 1 minute, or blanch them in boiling water for 1 minute. Toss with pasta, one finely chopped spring onion, a few shredded basil leaves and plenty of freshly ground black pepper. Add 2 tablespoons grated Parmesan cheese.
Calories 66

2 Grate 100 g/4 oz carrot and mix with 2 tablespoons orange juice. Add one chopped spring onion and toss with pasta. Serve with 25 g/1 oz grated mild Cheddar cheese.
Calories 151

3 Boil and roughly chop one egg. Sieve 25 g/1 oz cottage cheese and toss with the pasta. Add the egg, 3 tablespoons snipped chives and 3 tablespoons chopped fresh parsley. Season with a little grated nutmeg and freshly ground black pepper.
Calories 137

4 Melt 1 tablespoon butter in a pan and lightly scramble one egg until beginning to set. Toss with the pasta. Serve topped with 100 g/4 oz cooked fresh spinach. Sprinkle with freshly ground black pepper.
Calories 218

5 Peel, seed and roughly chop 50 g/2 oz tomatoes. Boil and roughly chop one egg. Toss the egg and tomatoes with the pasta, and season with pepper.
Calories 105

6 Dice 50 g/2 oz cooked chicken breast (without skin) and mix with 2 tablespoons thick yoghurt. Add freshly ground black pepper and 2 tablespoons snipped chives. Toss with the hot pasta.
Calories 140

7 Flake 25 g/1 oz tinned tuna in brine (drained) and toss with the pasta. Add a little lemon zest, 2 tablespoons chopped fresh parsley and a squeeze of lemon juice. Serve on a generous green salad.
Calories 50

8 Mix 3 tablespoons dry white wine, 100 g/4 oz sliced leek, one sliced celery stalk, one diced carrot and 100 g/4 oz shredded green cabbage in a saucepan. Cover and cook, shaking the pan often, for 15 minutes. Add 50 g/2 oz tomatoes, peeled and chopped, plenty of salt and pepper and cook, covered, for a further 15 minutes. Toss with the pasta and serve with one tablespoon grated Parmesan cheese.
Calories 139

9 Chop one garlic clove and mix with 1 teaspoon chopped fresh oregano and 25 g/1 oz chopped walnuts. Sieve 25 g/1 oz cottage cheese. Toss the garlic, oregano, walnuts and cottage cheese with the hot pasta.
Calories 231

10 Dice 25 g/1 oz lean cooked ham. Thinly slice 100 g/4 oz courgettes and toss with one teaspoon olive oil in a small saucepan. Cover and sweat the vegetables for 5 minutes. Toss the courgettes and ham with the pasta.
Calories 200

LIGHT PASTA AND LOW CALORIE COUNTS: SOME SERVING IDEAS

Here are a couple of suggestions for serving up calorie-controlled dishes that taste as good as they look.

- First, check the calorie content of the brand of pasta you are cooking.

- Always weigh the amount of pasta you are cooking per portion (check the package or table for details of this) so you can serve an amount for which the above calculation is easy.

MAKING PASTA AT HOME

Freshly made Italian pasta dough, quickly boiled and tossed with lots of melted butter or warmed olive oil, pepper, a little garlic and perhaps some chopped parsley or shredded basil, is delicious and simple to make. However, even though it is *possible* to make delicate Chinese-style won ton dough, the technique for making long oriental egg noodles is not one that is practical for the home cook to learn. The information that follows on mixing, kneading and boiling therefore applies to the Italian-style doughs, and specific notes and information are included with the various other basic pasta recipes.

Pasta is not difficult to make, but it does take a bit of kneading. Unlike delicate pastry, the dough is firm and glutinous, so some muscle power is required rather than the delicate touch practiced by pastry cooks. Strong flour is used for its gluten content, giving the dough its characteristic strength and texture, and allowing it to be rolled quite thinly with smooth results.

Useful equipment: slotted spoon; pasta boiler and colander; pasta machine and metal rolling pin

EQUIPMENT

If you already have a reasonably well-equipped kitchen, then you will not have to buy anything special for making pasta. However, if you have never tried making pasta before you may find the following points helpful.

A LARGE WORK SURFACE

This is something you do need for rolling out pasta dough. Make sure it is thoroughly clean and dry before you start. Unlike pastry making, you do want the pasta to 'adhere' to the surface slightly as you roll it, so it will pick up any grime!

ROLLING PIN

A rolling pin without knobs on the end is essential for pasta-making; otherwise you will end up with infuriating grooves running down the length of the pasta once you have rolled it out beyond a certain size.

Look out for rolling pins that have a central section that rotates on thin handles. As well as wooden ones, marble and stainless steel pins are good as they are easier to clean and they do not stick quite as easily.

Speciality kitchen stores sell extra-long pasta rolling pins but an average-length simpler implement is fine.

PASTRY WHEEL OR LARGE KNIFE

A pastry wheel is useful for cutting between filled and covered ravioli and it will give the pasta shapes an attractive fluted edge. However, a long-bladed cook's knife will also do the job efficiently.

RAVIOLI SHEET OR PAN

This is a small tray with indentations rather like a shallow muffin tin and a raised, serrated cutting edge between the indentations. The rolled-out pasta dough is laid over the pan and lightly pressed into the indentations, then the filling is added to these and the pasta is brushed with beaten egg between the dots of filling. A second sheet of pasta is applied on top and rolled with a rolling pin to separate the individual ravioli.

PASTA MACHINES

The most common and useful one for the average household is a hand-turned rolling machine. Small but heavy, the machine clamps to a work surface. The rollers may be set apart at different widths so that the dough can be rolled and folded several times instead of being kneaded by hand.

Cutting rollers can be fitted for making tagliatelle or linguine. A ravioli filler can also be attached. With this, folded sheets of pasta and the filling are fed in through a hopper, then the rollers do the job of filling and separating the individual pasta shapes. This is useful if you want to make very small pasta shapes, which are fiddly to manufacture by hand.

LARGE SAUCEPAN OR PASTA BOILER

It is worth investing in a very large saucepan that will have dozens of culinary uses apart from cooking pasta. Look out for a deep saucepan, complete with an integral strainer that fits snugly inside the pan to make maximum use of its capacity. Then, when the pasta is cooked, you simply lift out the perforated lining. This also prevents the pasta from sticking to the bottom of the pan.

LARGE COLANDER

A deep colander is essential for draining pasta well. A stainless steel colander can be placed back on top of the saucepan, which is extremely useful when you are juggling a colander of pasta and trying to add the finishing touches to a sauce.

KNEADING PASTA DOUGH BY MACHINE

If you have an electric pasta-maker, then follow the manufacturer's directions. The most popular type of pasta machine is the compact, hand-turned rolling machine. First, knead the dough by hand until it comes together in a fairly smooth ball. Then put this through the rollers and set to the widest setting. Fold the dough, press it together and roll it on the widest setting again. Repeat this process several times until the dough is smooth. This, clearly, is less tiring than kneading by hand and gives good results.

Once the dough is smooth, fold it and press it together into a neat lump, then place in a plastic bag and let sit for 15–30 minutes.

ROLLING OUT PASTA DOUGH

You can either roll the dough out by hand with a rolling pin or by machine. If you have a machine, then this stage is quick and easy. Simply pass the dough through the rollers, reducing the gap between them each time.

Work with a quantity of dough that you can handle easily. Unless you have a large kitchen table or work surface and a long pasta rolling pin, cut the complete batch of dough in half or quarters for rolling out. Keep the rest covered to prevent it drying out.

Press the dough into the shape required and lightly flour the surface before rolling it out. Try to keep the dough in the shape you want to end up with, pulling the corners out slightly as you work to make a square or rectangular shape or turning the dough to make a round.

Lift and turn the dough occasionally to prevent it sticking and keep the surface lightly floured. Do not dredge the surface heavily with flour, as this will dry the dough and make it more difficult to roll. Ideally, the dough should just cling to the surface as it is rolled. Once the dough is part-rolled and has been turned a couple of times, it becomes smooth and less likely to stick, so it is not necessary to flour the surface further. Lifting and shaking the dough slightly helps it keep its texture.

As you roll the dough – particularly if you are rolling it out with a rolling pin – look out for thick areas and concentrate on rolling them out to achieve an even result. It is easy to continue rolling in one direction so that the edges or one area of dough becomes far thinner than the middle or another area. Gently smoothing the dough with your hands occasionally helps and this is a good way of thinning any thick patches.

Pasta dough can be rolled out very thinly until you can see your hands through it, but this is not necessary. However, do not leave the dough thick as it makes the pasta noodles chewy and disappointingly stodgy. You should have to work fairly hard at rolling and stretching the dough without breaking its smooth surface, otherwise, the chances are that it is too thick. For noodles, the dough should be like thick brown paper or thin French crêpe after rolling.

If the time allows, leave the dough to rest for 10 minutes after rolling and before cutting. This relaxes the dough and helps to prevent it shrinking when cut, but it is not an essential process. If you do leave it to relax, make sure the surface underneath is dusted lightly with flour and cover with cling film.

Kneading the dough by machine.

CUTTING PASTA

CUTTING NOODLES BY MACHINE

This is a simple matter of changing the rollers to cut noodles. If you have rolled the pasta by hand, then the dough must be floured before cutting.

CUTTING NOODLES BY HAND

Sift a little flour over the dough and smooth it very lightly with the palm of your hand. Roll the dough up loosely, then cut it into strips as wide or as narrow as you want to make the noodles. Cut fine strips for linguine, 1 cm/½in-wide strips for tagliatelle or fettuccine, and 2.5 cm/1 in-wide strips for pappardelle.

As soon as you have cut the strips, shake out the pasta dough and place it on a plate dusted with flour

CUTTING LARGE SHAPES

Lasagne may be cut into squares measuring about 10 cm/4 in or into rectangular shapes measuring about 15 cm/6 in × 10 cm/4 in. However, when you make your own pasta you do not have to comply with the convention of always making square or rectangular lasagne.

The only point to consider when cutting large pieces of pasta is the size of the cooking container available.

CUTTING DECORATIVE SHAPES

Biscuit cutters and aspic cutters are ideal for stamping out decorative shapes. Flour the cutter occasionally to prevent the pasta sticking to it.

LASANKI

Lasanki are small pasta squares of Polish origin.

To make them, first cut the pasta dough into strips, then cut them across into squares – they should measure about ½–1 cm/¼–½ in on each side.

HAND-MADE BOWS

Cut strips of pasta, then cut these into short lengths and pinch them together in the middle to make bows. It is worth mentioning that although they are very good when home-made, it is a time-consuming process and the pasta tastes just as good in easier-to-make squares or diamond shapes!

PASTA DOUGH

INGREDIENTS
300 g/12 oz strong unbleached flour
1 tsp salt
3 eggs
4 tbsp olive oil
1 tbsp water

Mix the flour and salt together in a large bowl. Make a well in the middle, add the eggs, olive oil and water. Use a spoon to mix the eggs, oil and water, gradually working in the flour. When the mixture begins to bind together in clumps, scrape the spoon clean and knead the dough together with your hands.

Press the dough into a ball and roll it around the bowl to leave the bowl clean of mixture. Place the dough on a lightly floured, clean surface and knead thoroughly until smooth. Keep the dough moving and add extra flour to prevent sticking. Wrap in a plastic bag and leave to rest for 15–30 minutes. Do not chill or the dough will be difficult to handle.

Kneading the pasta dough by hand.

COOKING AND SERVING PASTA

COOKING PASTA

It is important for the greatest enjoyment of pasta that it is cooked correctly. It should be slightly firm with a bite to it, 'al dente' is the Italian expression. The only way to check whether pasta is cooked is by tasting. Fresh pasta cooks in about 3 minutes, although obviously it does depend on the type of pasta you are cooking. Dried pasta takes longer to cook; again the best way to check is by tasting. Filled pasta shapes can take longer depending on the filling, which may need cooking or heating through thoroughly. Read the instructions on the package when buying filled pasta.

As a general rule, allow 4 1/7 pts water to 450 g/1lb pasta. Use a large saucepan which will enable the pasta to move around in the water. Bring the water to a boil before adding any salt or the pasta. Use 1 tablespoon salt for 450 g/1 lb pasta. Add the salt as the water comes to the boil, then add the pasta all at once.

Immediately after the pasta has been added to the boiling water, stir to prevent it sticking to the pan. This will also help to submerge long strands of pasta. Put a lid on the pan to bring the water back to the boil as quickly as possible. Once the water has come back to the boil, remove the lid. Stir occasionally and taste until the pasta is cooked to 'al dente'.

COOKING PASTA SHEETS

Lasagne and large pieces of pasta really do have to be cooked in a large volume of water and with plenty of room for the water to boil rapidly. If the sheets are allowed to stay still in a small pan of water, they stick together and cook unevenly. If you do not have a very large saucepan, cook pasta sheets in batches.

DRAINING AND SERVING

Have a warmed serving dish ready to hold the cooked pasta. If the pasta is to be served plain, then you should have butter or warmed oil ready for dressing it. Freshly ground black pepper or grated Parmesan cheese may be added.

Drain the pasta as soon as it is cooked as a few extra minutes can ruin its texture, particularly in the case of fresh pasta.

Pasta sheets and tubes (cannelloni) should be rinsed under cold running water immediately after they are drained to prevent them cooking further. Then, they should be laid out on clean tea towels ready for use. If they are left folded in a colander, stacked or closed, they will stick together and become difficult to use.

Fresh pasta shapes

STORING AND FREEZING PASTA

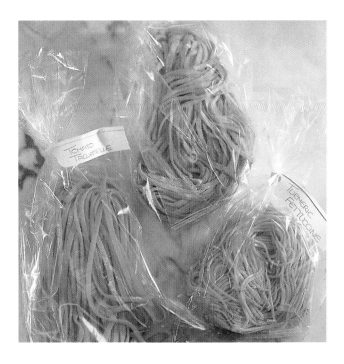

DRIED PASTA

Keep dried pasta in its sealed bag or in an airtight container, and use within the recommended period given on the package. Because of its long shelf-life, the pasta will not suddenly go off, but the flavour and texture will gradually deteriorate with prolonged storage past this date.

FRESH PASTA

This should be kept chilled and used within a couple of days of making. Always observe the recommended 'use by' date on packs.

COOKED PASTA

Plain, cooked pasta or cooked pasta dishes keep reasonably well, depending on the other ingredients used in them. Leftover cooked pasta or pasta that is cooked ahead for salads should be covered tightly to prevent it drying out, then kept in the refrigerator as soon as it has cooled.

The best method of reheating plain, cooked pasta is to do this in the microwave. It heats very quickly, you should follow the manufacturer's guidelines for how long to heat it for. Alternatively, place the covered dish of pasta over a saucepan of boiling water.

Sauced pasta can be reheated in the microwave, over a saucepan of boiling water or in the oven. When reheating pasta dishes in the oven, take care not to overcook them or to dry out the surface before the pasta is thoroughly reheated. As with any other food, when reheating pasta dishes make sure the whole batch of food is thoroughly heated throughout to its original cooking temperature before serving. Never reheat food more than once.

FREEZING PASTA

Uncooked fresh pasta freezes extremely well, and it can be cooked straight from frozen, allowing a nominally extra amount of time for tagliatelle and shapes, and slightly longer than this for filled pasta.

Ordinary cooked pasta does not freeze well. Although it is acceptable as a short-term measure for leftovers, which can be turned into a useful supper dish another time, it is not to be recommended as a method of cooking ahead for dinner parties and so on. This is also true of soups, hotpots or other very moist dishes (unthickened, stock-based sauces) that contain separate pieces of pasta. On thawing, the pasta is too soft and it breaks up easily.

Macaroni cheese and similar pasta dishes in which the pasta is protected by a fairly thick sauce have slightly better freezing qualities, however. Also, baked dishes containing sheets or similar large areas of pasta, such as lasagne or cannelloni, freeze very well.

DRESSINGS AND SAUCES

ANCHOVY AND EGG CREAM SAUCE

Serves 4

This sauce is quick to prepare for unexpected guests, especially if you keep some cream in the freezer. Good with spaghetti, noodles or shapes, and ideal in small quantities for a first course.

INGREDIENTS

8 eggs

50 g/2 oz tin anchovy fillets

4 spring onions, chopped

350 ml/12 fl oz single cream

freshly ground black pepper

plenty of shredded basil or chopped
fresh parsley

Place the eggs in a saucepan and cover with cold water. Bring to the boil, then cook for 8 minutes. Meanwhile, drain the oil from the anchovies into a small pan. Add the spring onions and cook for 2 minutes. Chop the anchovy fillets, add them to the spring onions, then stir in the cream and add pepper to taste. Heat very gently but do not allow to simmer or the cream will curdle.

Shell and roughly chop the hard-boiled eggs, then mix them into the sauce with the fresh basil or parsley. Serve at once, tossed into the freshly cooked, drained pasta.

TONNATO DRESSING

Serves 4

Tonnato is a cold sauce which is traditionally served with cold cooked veal;
however, this versatile tuna mayonnaise is excellent on freshly cooked pasta of any type.

INGREDIENTS

2 egg yolks

juice of 1 lemon

salt and freshly ground black pepper

200 g/7 oz tin tuna in oil

scant olive oil

125 g/5 oz soured cream or thick
yoghurt (optional)

2 tbsp capers, chopped

chopped fresh parsley, to serve

Place the egg yolks in a bowl. Use an electric beater to whisk in the lemon juice and a little seasoning. Whisk in the oil drained from the tin of tuna. Whisking all the time on high speed, trickle in the olive oil very slowly. If you add the oil too quickly, the mixture will curdle; however, once it begins to thicken into a creamy mayonnaise, the oil can be poured in more quickly.

Mash the tuna fish to a paste, then mix it into the mayonnaise. Stir in the cream or yoghurt (if used), and the capers. (The cream or yoghurt lighten the sauce slightly.) Taste for seasoning before serving and sprinkle the freshly cooked, drained pasta and sauce with chopped parsley.

Anchovy and Egg Cream Sauce ▶

SAUSAGE MEATBALL SAUCE

Serves 4

This sauce is simple to prepare, although if you are in a hurry you could always use ready-seasoned sausage meat.
Serve with ribbon noodles.

INGREDIENTS

450 g/1 lb pork sausage meat

1 onion, finely chopped

1 garlic clove, crushed

¼ tsp chilli powder

1 tsp ground coriander

salt and freshly ground black pepper

1 tsp dried oregano

1 tsp chopped fresh thyme

1 tbsp chopped fresh sage

150 g/6 oz fresh breadcrumbs

1 egg

1 tbsp oil

1 green pepper, seeded and diced

150 g/6 oz button mushrooms

½ quantity Good Tomato Sauce
(page 40)

Place the sausage meat in a bowl. Add the onion, garlic, chilli, coriander, seasoning, oregano, thyme, sage and breadcrumbs. Use a mixing spoon to break up the sausage meat and mix in some of the other ingredients. When the sausage meat is well broken up, add the egg. Then pound the ingredients together until thoroughly combined.

Wash your hands, then rinse them under cold water and keep them wet whilst you shape the meatballs to prevent the mixture sticking to them. Shape small, walnut-sized meatballs.

Heat the oil in a large frying pan. Add the meatballs and brown them all over, using a spoon and fork to roll them around the frying pan. Add the green pepper and mushrooms, and continue to cook for 10 minutes, or until the pepper is softened slightly. Pour in the tomato sauce and bring to the boil. Simmer for 20 minutes, turning the meatballs in the sauce occasionally. Serve piping hot.

AUBERGINE AND LEEK TOPPING

Serves 4

This deliciously creamy sauce is more healthy than it looks. The richness comes from the combination of aubergines and tahini, which is available from most health-food stores.

INGREDIENTS

2 large aubergines, trimmed and cubed

salt and freshly ground black pepper

about 4 tbsp olive oil

2 garlic cloves, crushed

¼ tsp chilli powder

450 g/1 lb leeks, sliced

2 tbsp tahini

425 ml/15 fl oz stock (vegetable or chicken)

Place the aubergines in a strainer and sprinkle them with salt, then leave them to stand over a bowl for 20 minutes. Rinse the aubergines well and leave to drain.

Heat half the olive oil in a large saucepan. Add some of the aubergine cubes and brown them on all sides. Use a slotted spoon to remove the cubes from the pan and set aside. Add more oil as necessary and cook the remaining cubes. Set aside. Add the garlic, chilli powder and leeks to the pan, then cook, stirring often, for 10 minutes until the leeks are greatly reduced in volume.

Replace the aubergine cubes and stir in the tahini, then pour in the vegetable or chicken stock and bring to the boil. Reduce the heat and cover the pan, then simmer for 15–20 minutes, until the aubergines and leeks are cooked through. Taste for seasoning before serving.

Broccoli and Baby Corn Dressing

Serves 4

Steaming and stir-frying the vegetables in this dressing makes it both quick and healthy to prepare.
Serve with spaghetti or noodles.

INGREDIENTS

450 g/1 lb broccoli, cut into small florets

225 g/8 oz whole baby corn cobs

2 tbsp butter or 2 tbsp oil

1 onion, chopped

100 g/4 oz diced bacon

1 tbsp plain flour

salt and freshly ground black pepper

90 ml/4 fl oz dry sherry

180 ml/7 fl oz chicken or vegetable stock

freshly grated Parmesan cheese, to serve

Place the broccoli in a steamer and cook over boiling water for 5 minutes. Add the baby corn cobs and cook for a further 5 minutes. Alternatively, cook the vegetables for the same time in the minimum of boiling water; they have a better flavor if they are steamed.

Melt the butter or heat the oil in a large saucepan. Add the onion and bacon, and cook, stirring often, until both are cooked. Stir in the flour and a little seasoning, then add the sherry and stock. Stir in the broccoli and corn. Bring to a boil, reduce the heat, and cover the pan. Simmer for 5 minutes. Taste for seasoning.

Serve the broccoli and baby corn cobs and their sauce tossed into freshly cooked, drained pasta. Offer Parmesan cheese and extra ground pepper at the table.

PUMPKIN SAUCE

Serves 4

This brightly-colored sauce, served with herb tagliatelle or shapes, would be perfect for a family thanksgiving supper. For the best taste, make sure you do not overcook the pumpkin.

INGREDIENTS

3 tbsp olive oil

2 large onions, chopped

1 garlic clove, crushed

1 bay leaf

2 tbsp chopped fresh sage

1 tsp dried marjoram

900 g/2 lb pumpkin, seeded, peeled and cubed

salt and freshly ground black pepper

75 g/3 oz button mushrooms, sliced

2 × 400 g/14 oz tins chopped tomatoes

2 tbsp chopped fresh parsley

freshly grated Parmesan cheese, to

Heat the oil in a large saucepan. Add the onions, garlic, bay leaf, sage and marjoram. Cook, stirring, for 5 minutes, then add the pumpkin and mix well. Sprinkle in seasoning and continue to cook, stirring often, for 5 minutes. Stir in the mushrooms and tomatoes, heat until simmering and cover the pan. Cook gently for 35–40 minutes, until the pumpkin is tender but not mushy.

Stir in the chopped fresh parsley and taste for seasoning before serving, ladled over tagliatelle or other pasta shapes. Offer Parmesan cheese with the pumpkin sauce and freshly cooked, drained pasta.

PEPPER SAUCE

Serves 4–6

Most of the ingredients for this Mediterranean-style sauce can be found in your larder. It is simple to prepare and should take about a half an hour to make, at most.

INGREDIENTS

4 tbsp olive oil

2 garlic cloves, finely chopped

225 g/8 oz rindless bacon slices, diced

1 onion, halved and thinly sliced

2 red peppers, seeded, quartered lengthwise and cut in strips

2 green peppers, seeded, quartered lengthwise and cut in strips

25 g/1 oz pine nuts

6 tbsp raisins

salt and freshly ground black pepper

180 ml/7 fl oz dry sherry

Heat the oil in a large frying pan. Add the garlic, bacon, onion and red and green peppers. Cook, stirring often, for 5 minutes. Stir in the pine nuts and raisins with plenty of seasoning, then continue to cook, stirring occasionally, for 15 minutes.

Pour in the sherry and bring to the boil. Boil for 3 minutes. Taste and adjust the seasoning before pouring the sauce over freshly cooked, drained pasta. Toss well and serve at once.

Wonderful Mushroom Sauce

Serves 4

Look out for dried mushrooms in Italian and Eastern European delicatessens. This rich sauce, combining dried and fresh mushrooms, is delicious with plain noodles.

INGREDIENTS

2 whole dried mushrooms

180 ml/7 fl oz boiling water

2 tbsp butter

1 tbsp olive oil

½ small onion, finely chopped

1 bay leaf

225 g/9 oz button mushrooms, sliced

150 ml/¼ pint dry sherry

salt and freshly ground black pepper

300 g/12 oz oyster mushrooms

300 ml/½ pint single cream

3 tbsp chopped fresh parsley

1 tbsp lemon juice

Heat the butter and oil in a frying pan. Add the onion and bay leaf, then cook, stirring, for 5 minutes. Add the sliced button mushrooms and continue to cook for 15–20 minutes. The mushrooms will give up their liquor and shrink: this stage is complete when all the liquid has evaporated, leaving the darkened mushrooms in the oil and butter, and it is important for a good flavour. Add the dried mushrooms and the strained liquid. Stir in the sherry and seasoning, then simmer for 5 minutes.

Add the oyster mushrooms and poach them in the sauce for 3 minutes, so that they are hot and lightly cooked. Stir in the single cream, chopped fresh parsley and lemon juice. Heat gently without boiling. Taste for seasoning and serve ladled over freshly cooked, drained noodle pasta.

P lace the dried mushrooms in a small bowl and add the boiling water. Put a saucer on the mushrooms to keep them submerged and leave to soak for 15 minutes. Place the mushrooms and the liquid in a small saucepan and simmer for 10 minutes, adding a little extra water if necessary. Drain, reserving the cooking liquor. Chop the mushrooms. Strain the liquor through a muslin-lined strainer to remove any grit.

GOOD TOMATO SAUCE

Serves 4–6

Good fresh pasta and a rich tomato sauce, topped with some freshly grated Parmesan cheese, is a simple yet splendid meal, particularly if there is a really fresh, crisp green salad as an accompaniment. This sauce also has many uses in baked dishes or with stuffed pasta.

INGREDIENTS

2 tbsp olive oil

I large onion, chopped

I carrot, chopped

I celery stalk, chopped

I garlic clove, crushed

I bay leaf

2 thyme sprigs

4 parsley sprigs

I tbsp all-purpose flour

2 tbsp tomato purée

900 g/2 lb ripe tomatoes, roughly chopped

I tbsp caster sugar

180 ml/7 fl oz dry red wine

salt and freshly ground black pepper

freshly grated Parmesan cheese, to serve

Heat the oil in a large, heavy-based saucepan. Add the onion, carrot, celery, garlic, bay leaf, thyme and parsley. Cook, stirring, for 10 minutes, until the onion is softened slightly but not browned. Stir in the flour and tomato purée.

Then add the tomatoes and sugar and stir in the wine. Add some seasoning, bring to the boil and give the sauce a good stir. Reduce the heat, cover the pan and leave to simmer for I hour.

Remove the bay leaf and herb sprigs, then purée the sauce in a blender and sieve to remove the seeds. Re-heat and taste for seasoning before serving. Ladle the sauce over freshly cooked, drained pasta and top with Parmesan cheese.

WHITE WINE SAUCE

Makes 675 g/1½ lb

An elegant sauce that is best served with delicate ingredients such as smoked salmon or wild mushrooms.
It is quick and easy to prepare.

INGREDIENTS

50 g/2 oz butter

1 small onion, finely chopped

1 bay leaf

2 parsley sprigs with long stems

40 g/1½ oz button mushrooms, thinly sliced

40 g/1½ oz plain flour

300 ml/½ pint dry white wine

180 ml/7 fl oz stock (chicken, vegetable or fish, depending on the dish)

salt and freshly ground white or black pepper

50 ml/2 fl oz single cream

Melt the butter in a saucepan. Add the chopped onion, bay leaf and parsley sprigs, then cook, stirring often, for 15 minutes until the onion is softened slightly but not browned. Stir in the sliced button mushrooms, then stir in the flour. Gradually stir in the white wine and stock, then bring to the boil. The sauce will be too thick at this stage. Cover the pan tightly and allow the sauce to cook very gently for 15 minutes.

Add seasoning and beat the sauce well. Remove the bay leaf and parsley sprigs. Stir in the cream and heat gently without boiling.

PASTA WITH PEPPER SAUCE AND OLIVES

Serves 4

This low-fat pepper sauce helps to keep the calories in this dish down. As long as the pasta used is dairy-free, this dish is also suitable for vegans.

INGREDIENTS

450 g/1 lb dried rigatoni

dash of olive oil

40 g/1½ oz stoned black olives, roughly chopped

grated Cheddar cheese, to serve

PEPPER SAUCE

2 red peppers, skinned, seeded and roughly chopped

4 garlic cloves, peeled

300 ml/½ pint vegetable stock

salt and freshly ground black pepper

Bring a large saucepan of water to the boil, and add the rigatoni with a dash of olive oil. Cook for about 10 minutes, stirring occasionally, until tender. Drain and return to the saucepan. Set aside.

To make the sauce, place the chopped peppers, garlic and stock in a food processor or blender, and season with salt and freshly ground black pepper. Purée until smooth.

Stir the pepper sauce into the rigatoni with the chopped olives. Serve with grated Cheddar cheese.

Béchamel Sauce

Makes about 675 g/1½ lb

Well-cooked, good-quality pasta makes a delicious meal with the minimum of additions: in the Italian kitchen, that means olive oil and garlic or butter with Parmesan; to the traditional American or British cook, a good milk-based sauce is popular too. Béchamel is used in a variety of pasta dishes, notably as the topping for baked lasagne.

INGREDIENTS

1 thick onion slice
1 bay leaf
1 mace blade
2 parsley sprigs
600 ml/1 pint milk
3 tbsp butter
40 g/1½ oz plain flour
salt and freshly ground white or black pepper

Place the onion, bay leaf, mace and parsley in a saucepan. Add the milk and heat slowly until just boiling. Remove from the heat, cover and leave for 45 minutes.

Strain the milk into a jug or bowl. Wash the saucepan, then melt the butter and stir in the flour. Slowly pour in the milk, stirring all the time. Continue stirring until the sauce boils, then reduce the heat, if necessary, so that it just simmers. Cook for 3 minutes, stirring occasionally. Add seasoning to taste.

If the sauce is not used straight away, lay a piece of dampened greaseproof paper directly on its surface to prevent a skin forming.

VARIATIONS

Any one of the following may be mixed with freshly cooked pasta and served as a light meal.
A gratin topping may be added by sprinkling the sauced pasta with fresh breadcrumbs mixed with
2 tablespoons freshly grated Parmesan cheese and browning in the grill.

Cheese Sauce Stir in grated sharp tasting Cheddar cheese and 4 tablespoons freshly grated Parmesan cheese after the Béchamel sauce has simmered.

Egg Sauce Hardboil and roughly chop 6 eggs, then mix them into the cooked Béchamel sauce. Add 1 tablespoon chopped fresh tarragon or parsley, or 2 tablespoons chopped dill, if preferred.

Mushroom Sauce Add sliced button mushrooms before the final simmering.

Onion Sauce Finely chop 2 large onions. Cook them in the butter for about 20 minutes, stirring often, until they are softened. Do not allow the onions to brown but do make sure that they are well cooked, otherwise the sauce will be inferior. Stir in the flour and continue as above.

Tuna Sauce Drain a 225 g/7-ounce tin of tuna. Flake the fish and add it to the sauce before the final simmering. Add 2 tablespoons of chopped parsley and 1 tablespoon of chopped capers.

Tuna may be added to a mushroom sauce, or an onion sauce may be prepared, then both mushrooms and tuna added. The oil from the tin may be used instead of butter.

PASTA WITH OIL AND GARLIC

Serves 4

Good-quality olive oil and plump fresh garlic turn a plate of fresh pasta into a positive feast of a snack! You can increase the quantities of oil and garlic to suit your taste and serve with freshly grated Parmesan if you like.

INGREDIENTS

125–150 ml/4½–5 fl oz olive oil

4 garlic cloves, chopped

freshly ground black pepper

450 g/1 lb fresh tagliatelle or spaghetti

Heat the olive oil and chopped garlic in a small saucepan. Cook the garlic very gently for 2 minutes – it should not fry rapidly, simply give up its flavor to the oil. Toss the oil and garlic and freshly ground black pepper into the freshly cooked, drained pasta. Serve at once.

PESTO

Makes about 600 ml/1 pint

This is a wonderfully aromatic sauce based on basil.

Although pesto is traditionally made by pounding all the ingredients using a pestle and mortar, a food processor or blender is more or less essential for the busy cook. If you do not have either, then work in far smaller quantities than those given below.

INGREDIENTS

150 g/6 oz fresh Parmesan cheese, rind removed

100 g/4 oz pine nuts

4 garlic cloves

150 g/6 oz basil sprigs (soft stems and leaves only; discard tough stalks before weighing)

375–450 ml/13 fl oz–¾ pint good-quality virgin olive oil

salt and freshly ground black pepper

Break the Parmesan into small pieces and place in the food processor with the pine nuts and garlic. Process the mixture until the Parmesan is finely crumbled. Add the basil and continue processing until the herb is chopped and the mixture begins to clump together into a coarse, bright-green paste.

Add a little of the olive oil and process the mixture until it is incorporated, then gradually trickle in the remaining olive oil. Add enough to make a thin, pouring paste. Add seasoning to taste.

If using a blender, process the mixture in batches. The oil does not form a mayonnaise-like liaison; it will separate on standing and the paste has to be stirred again. Mix all the batches together at the end so that the ingredients are combined in the correct proportions.

Top individual portions of freshly cooked, drained pasta with a couple of spoonfuls of pesto, then toss together and eat at once – delicious!

SUN-DRIED TOMATO AND VERMOUTH SPECIAL

Serves 4

You can keep a jar of the dressing in the refrigerator for a couple of weeks for emergency pasta snacks!

INGREDIENTS

12 sun-dried tomatoes

200 ml/⅓ pint dry white vermouth

1 bay leaf

1 large marjoram sprig

150 ml/¼ pint olive oil

450 g/1 lb fresh small pasta squares, fusilli or broken spaghetti

freshly ground black pepper

1 red or white onion, very thinly sliced and separated into rings

freshly grated Parmesan cheese, to serve

Use a pair of kitchen scissors to snip the tomatoes into strips, then across into small pieces. Do this over a large screw-top jar. Add the vermouth, bay leaf and marjoram, then pour in the oil and cover the jar. Shake well and leave to stand for at least 3 hours – the longer the better, ideally overnight.

Tip the tomato mixture into a small saucepan and heat fairly slowly until just boiling. Reduce the heat so that the mixture barely bubbles and leave whilst you cook the pasta. Stir the tomatoes occasionally, then stir well just before pouring over the piping hot, drained pasta. Add the freshly ground black pepper and toss the pasta to coat all the pieces with the dressing. Top with the onion rings and serve with Parmesan cheese.

Fusilli with Tomato and Chilli Sauce

Serves 4–6

Always wear gloves when preparing chillies and be careful not to touch your eyes accidentally as they will really sting!

INGREDIENTS

2 garlic cloves, crushed

1 medium onion, sliced

900 g/2 lb fresh or tinned plum
tomatoes

1 tsp sugar

2 tsp finely chopped fresh basil

2 fresh chillies

450 g/1 lb fresh fusilli

Make a tomato sauce, using the garlic, onion, tomatoes, sugar and basil as for Spaghetti Morgan (see page 146).

As the sauce is cooking, slice and seed the chillies. Add them to the sauce 5 minutes before you are ready to serve it.

Toss the sauce with the freshly cooked, drained fusilli.

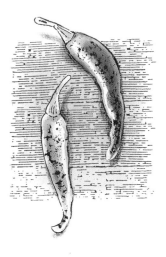

PASTA AL POMODORO

Serves 4–6

Any pasta shape would be suitable for this recipe, so use whatever you have in the cupboard. The sauce is quick and simple, making this dish a perfect supper for unexpected guests.

INGREDIENTS

450 g/1 lb dried pasta

dash of olive oil

2 tbsp butter

2 garlic cloves, crushed

1 onion, chopped

225 g/8 oz sieved tomatoes

salt and freshly ground black pepper

fresh flat parsley sprigs, to garnish

shaved fresh Parmesan cheese, to serve

Bring a saucepan of water to the boil and add the pasta with a dash of olive oil. Cook for about 10 minutes, stirring occasionally, until tender. Drain and set aside, covered, to keep warm.

Melt the butter in a large frying pan and sauté the garlic and onion for about 3 minutes, until softened. Stir in the tomatoes and season with salt and freshly ground black pepper. Simmer the sauce for about 10 minutes, then serve with the pasta, garnished with parsley sprigs and sprinkled with shaved, fresh Parmesan cheese.

SALMON WITH DILL AND MUSTARD

Serves 4

Although delicate, salmon is a rich fish and the piquancy of this mustard sauce complements it perfectly. For classic simplicity, arrange the fish and its dressing on home-made egg noodles, or add a zesty note to the pasta by mixing the zest of one lemon with the flour when mixing the dough. The dill must be fresh – forget the recipe if you only have dried dillweed as it will make the sauce taste as though you have used grass cuttings.

INGREDIENTS

675–900 g/1½–2 lb salmon fillet, skinned

salt and freshly ground black pepper

4 tbsp olive oil

1 tbsp lemon juice

½ onion, finely chopped

180 ml/6.5 fl oz milk

2 tbsp all-purpose flour

4 tbsp Dijon or other mild mustard

150 g/6 oz soured cream

3 tbsp chopped dill

¼ cucumber, peeled and finely diced

1 celery stalk, finely diced

Lay the salmon on a large piece of double-thick foil. Season it really well, then sprinkle with 1 tablespoon of the oil and the lemon juice. Grill the fish for about 15 minutes, or until cooked through.

Meanwhile, heat the remaining oil in a saucepan and add the onion. Cook, stirring, for 10 minutes. Stir in the flour and cook for 3 minutes before stirring in the milk, then bring to the boil. Beat the mustard into the thick sauce, then stir in the cream and heat gently but do not boil. Finally, stir in the dill and remove from the heat, then taste for seasoning.

Mix the cucumber and celery. Drain the cooking liquid from the salmon into the sauce. Use two forks to separate the cooked salmon into large chunks. Mix the mustard and dill sauce into the freshly cooked, drained pasta, then lightly mix in the fish. Divide between serving platters and top each portion with a little of the cucumber and celery.

SEAFOOD MEDLEY

Serves 4

You can vary the mixture of seafood according to your budget, the choice at the fishmongers and personal preference. Remember to add delicate ingredients at the end so they do not overcook. Serve with plain pasta or try combining a mixture of tomato, spinach and plain pasta.

INGREDIENTS

900 g/2 lb mussels

1 bay leaf

300 ml/½ pint dry white wine

6 tbsp olive oil

1 onion, halved and thinly sliced

1 celery stalk, finely diced

1 green pepper, seeded and finely diced

3 garlic cloves, crushed

zest of 1 lemon

salt and freshly ground black pepper

4 small squid, cleaned and sliced

300 g/12 oz goosefish fillet, cut in small chunks

6–8 scallops, shelled and sliced

300 g/12 oz peeled cooked prawns, thawed if frozen

8 black olives, stoned and chopped

plenty of chopped fresh parsley

freshly grated Parmesan cheese, to serve

Scrub the mussels and scrape off any barnacles or dirt on the shell. Pull away the black beard which protrudes from the shell. Discard any open mussels which do not shut when tapped. Place the mussels in a large pan and add the bay leaf and wine. Bring to the boil, then put a close-fitting lid on the pan and reduce the heat slightly so that the wine does not boil too rapidly. Cook for about 10 minutes, shaking the pan often, until all the mussels are open. Discard any that are shut. Strain the mussels, reserving the cooking liquor and bay leaf. Reserve a few mussels for garnish, if you like, and use a fork to remove the others from their shells.

Heat the oil in a large saucepan. Add the reserved bay leaf, sliced onion, diced celery, green pepper, garlic, lemon zest and season with plenty of salt and freshly ground black pepper. Cover and cook, stirring occasionally, for 20 minutes, or until the onion is softened but not browned. Pour in the reserved cooking liquor, bring to the boil, and boil hard for about 3 minutes, or until reduced by half. Then reduce the heat and add the squid. Cover the pan and simmer for 5 minutes. Add the goosefish, cover the pan again, and cook for a further 5 minutes. Next, add the scallops and cook gently for 3 minutes, or until the seafood is just cooked.

Add the prawns, mussels and olives. Heat gently, then taste for seasoning. Stir in plenty of parsley and serve at once, sprinkled with Parmesan cheese over the seafood and freshly cooked, drained pasta.

PIQUANT PRAWN AND TOMATO SAUCE

Serves 4

Good with spaghetti or noodles, this sauce may also be
layered with lasagne, then covered with a creamy topping and baked.

INGREDIENTS

2 tbsp oil
2 garlic cloves, crushed
2 green chillies, seeded and chopped
1 large onion, chopped
1 green pepper, seeded and diced
1 carrot, diced
2 celery stalks, diced
1 bay leaf
2 × 400 g/14 oz tins chopped tomatoes
1 tbsp tomato purée
1 tsp sugar
salt and freshly ground black pepper
450 g/1 lb frozen peeled cooked prawns
2 tbsp chopped fresh coriander

Heat the oil in a large saucepan and cook the garlic, green chillies, chopped onion, green pepper, carrot, celery and bay leaf, stirring, for 20 minutes. Stir in the chopped tomatoes, tomato purée, sugar and plenty of seasoning. Bring to the boil, reduce the heat, cover and simmer gently for 30 minutes.

Add the prawns, stir well and cook for 15 minutes, or until they are hot through. Taste for seasoning, then ladle the sauce over freshly cooked, drained pasta and top with the coriander.

SMOKED FISH HOTPOT

Serves 4

Smoked fish tastes really good with pasta. I have used fusilli here,
but shells or other shapes that cook reasonably quickly may be used.

INGREDIENTS

2 tbsp olive oil

1 large onion, halved and thinly sliced

1 red pepper, seeded and sliced

zest of 1 lemon

2 tbsp all-purpose flour

875 ml/30 fl oz fish stock

salt and freshly ground black pepper

225 g/8 oz fresh fusilli

700 g/1½ lb smoked fish fillet, skinned

2 tbsp butter (optional)

4 eggs, hard-boiled and roughly chopped

Heat the olive oil in a flameproof casserole or heavy-based saucepan and cook the onion, pepper and lemon peel, stirring occasionally, for 10 minutes. Stir in the flour, then slowly pour in the stock. Add salt and pepper, and bring to the boil, stirring all the time. Add the pasta, then reduce the heat so that the sauce simmers.

Place the smoked fish fillet on a suitable plate to cover the pan. Top with the 2 tablespoons of butter if using and cover with a saucepan lid or aluminium foil. Put the fish on top of the pan in place of its lid and simmer gently for 20–30 minutes, or until the pasta is cooked. Stir occasionally to prevent the pasta sticking.

Flake the fish, discarding the skin, and any bones. Lightly mix it into the pasta with all the butter from steaming (if used) and the hard-boiled eggs. Taste for seasoning and serve at once.

SIMPLE FISH SAUCE

Serves 4

This is an ideal way to cook frozen fish fillets or steaks. Smoked fish can be used instead of regular white fish
for a little variety and cooked seafood, such as peeled cooked prawns, can be added to the sauce for extra texture and
flavour. Serve the sauce on a bed of tagliatelle verde or on fettuccine flavoured with squid ink.
This is a sauce that can be served with any pasta you like.

INGREDIENTS

700 g/1½ lb cod fillet

1 bay leaf

600 ml/1 pint milk

3 tbsp butter

1 small onion, finely chopped

1 small carrot, finely diced

6 tbsp plain flour

150 g/6 oz button mushrooms, sliced

1 tbsp horseradish sauce (optional)

3 tbsp chopped fresh parsley

1 tbsp chopped capers

salt and freshly ground black pepper

freshly grated Parmesan cheese,
to serve

Place the cod in a saucepan or deep frying pan, add the bay leaf, and pour in the milk. Heat gently until the milk is just coming to simmering point. Then, remove from the heat and leave to cool.

When the fish has cooled, lift it carefully from the milk and flake the flesh off the skin in large pieces.

Reserve the milk.

Melt the butter in a saucepan, add the onion and carrot and stir well. Cover and cook for 15 minutes, until the onion has softened.

Whilst this is cooking, strain the reserved milk.

Stir the flour into the onion mixture, then stir in the milk and bring the sauce to the boil. Add the mushrooms and cook gently, stirring,

for 3 minutes. The liquor from the mushrooms will thin the sauce slightly.

Add the horseradish sauce, chopped parsley, capers, salt and ground black pepper to the sauce and taste it to check the seasoning. Then add the fish. Cook gently for 2–3 minutes, until the fish is hot. Serve at once, offering freshly grated Parmesan cheese with the sauce and freshly cooked, drained pasta.

SMOKED MACKEREL WITH HORSERADISH CREAM

Serves 4

This is a mixture to toss with pasta, rather than to pour over it.

INGREDIENTS

2 tbsp butter

I small onion, chopped

75 g/3 oz button mushrooms, sliced

450 g/I lb smoked mackerel fillet, skinned and flaked

4 tbsp horseradish sauce

300 ml/½ pint single cream

2 tbsp chopped fresh dill

salt and freshly ground black pepper

Melt the butter in a saucepan and cook the onion, stirring for about 10 minutes or until the onion has softened but not browned. Stir in the mushrooms and cook for a further 5 minutes.

Add the flaked mackerel and heat gently. Stir in the horseradish sauce, single cream and chopped dill with salt and pepper to taste. Heat the sauce gently without boiling. Toss the sauce with freshly cooked, drained pasta and serve at once.

SPAGHETTI WITH CLAMS

Serves 4

Parmesan cheese is traditionally served with Italian seafood dishes, and this one is no exception.

INGREDIENTS

450 g/I lb fresh spaghetti

salt to taste

225 g/½ lb fresh clams

2 tbsp olive oil

I garlic clove, crushed

I medium onion, finely sliced

2 anchovy fillets, chopped

400 g/14 oz plum or tinned tomatoes, roughly chopped

I tbsp finely chopped fresh parsley

freshly ground black pepper

Cook the pasta in the usual way. The sauce will take about 25 minutes, so begin cooking the pasta about 5–10 minutes later.

Put the clams in a pot with a close-fitting lid. Sweat them over a medium heat for 3–4 minutes. Remove from the heat and discard any that have failed to open. Detach the rest from their shells, rinse them to remove any sand and set aside. Strain the clam juices left in the pot and add them to the bowl with clams.

Heat the olive oil and cook the crushed garlic and sliced onion for 3–4 minutes to soften, without allowing them to colour. Add the anchovy fillets and tomatoes. Cook the sauce for about 15 minutes.

When the pasta is cooked, drain and set on a warm serving dish. Turn the flame under the sauce to high and, as it begins to split, add the fresh clams and the finely chopped fresh parsley. Check the salt, add ground black pepper and pour over the pasta.

MUSSELS IN LEMON-CREAM SAUCE

Serves 4

Ladle this flavoursome sauce over bowls of freshly cooked pasta shells.
Serve with plenty of crusty bread to mop up the juices.

INGREDIENTS

900 g/2 lb fresh mussels

300 ml/½ pint dry white wine

2 bay leaves

pared peel of 1 lemon

2 tbsp butter

1 garlic clove, finely chopped

1 small onion, finely chopped

1 celery stalk, diced

1 tbsp plain flour

salt and freshly ground black pepper

1 egg yolk

300 ml/½ pint single cream

2 tbsp chopped fresh dill

2 tbsp chopped fresh parsley

freshly grated Romano or Parmesan
cheese to serve

Prepare the fresh mussels by removing the beards and scraping them thoroughly.

Slowly heat the wine, bay leaves and lemon peel in a large saucepan until boiling. Add the mussels and bring the wine to the boil, then reduce the heat and cover the pan. Cook for about 10 minutes, shaking the pan occasionally, until all the mussels are open (discard any that do not open). Remove from the heat and shell the mussels, reserving a few in their shells if liked for garnishing.

Strain the cooking liquid from the mussels through fine muslin. Remove the lemon peel and cut it into fine shreds. Discard the bay leaves.

Heat the butter in a saucepan and add the garlic, onion, celery and lemon peel. Stir well, cover the pan, then cook for 15 minutes or until the vegetables have softened.

Stir in the flour, then gradually stir in the strained cooking liquor and bring to the boil, stirring. Simmer for 3 minutes. Season to taste.

Add the mussels and heat gently without boiling. Beat the egg yolk with the cream. Stir in a ladleful of hot sauce, then pour the mixture back into the saucepan and heat without allowing the sauce to simmer. Stir in the dill and parsley and serve, offering Romano or Parmesan cheese separately. If you have reserved some mussels in their shells, use them to garnish the plates of pasta and sauce.

SCALLOPS IN VEGETABLE SAUCE

Serves 4

Scallops have a beautiful fan-shaped shell that you can use to serve this dish. Fresh scallops should have a sweet
smell and a moist sheen. This fresh-tasting recipe makes an excellent supper dish or appetizer.
Use halved scallops or thickly sliced, if large.

INGREDIENTS

2 tbsp butter

1 tbsp olive oil

1 leek, sliced

100 g/4 oz broccoli, divided into small
florets

25 g/1 oz plain flour

300 ml/½ pint fish stock

300 ml/½ pint dry white wine

salt and freshly ground black pepper

225 g/8 oz mange tout

12 fresh scallops

25 g/1 oz grated Parmesan cheese

4 basil sprigs, shredded

Heat the butter and oil in a saucepan. Add the leek and broccoli, then cook for 5 minutes or until reduced in volume. Stir in the flour, then slowly pour in the fish stock and wine and bring to the boil, stirring. Add a little salt and pepper, then simmer uncovered for 3 minutes.

Add the mange tout and simmer for a further 3 minutes. Then, add the scallops and continue to cook gently, below simmering point, for about 5 minutes or until the scallops are just firm (do not allow the sauce to bubble rapidly or the scallops will toughen quickly).

Stir in the Parmesan and taste for seasoning, then add the basil and serve at once.

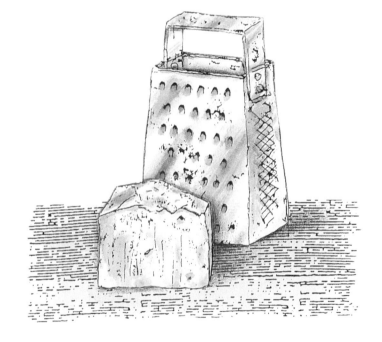

TUNA TRIANGLES

Serves 6–8

Serve these tasty triangles with Good Tomato Sauce (page 40) or White Wine Sauce (page 42).

INGREDIENTS

200 g/7 oz tin tuna, drained

2 tbsp finely chopped scallions

1 garlic clove, crushed

100 g/4 oz fresh white breadcrumbs

zest of ½ lemon

4 tbsp freshly grated Parmesan cheese

salt and freshly ground black pepper

about 3 tbsp milk

⅔ quantity Pasta Dough (page 27)

1 egg, beaten

freshly grated Parmesan cheese, to serve

Mash the tuna, then mix in the scallions, garlic and breadcrumbs. Add the lemon peel, Parmesan cheese and seasoning to taste. Mix in just enough milk to bind the mixture.

Roll out half the pasta dough into a 30 cm/12 in square. Cut it into 5 × 12.5 cm//5 in × 6cm/2½ in strips, then cut these across into squares. Brush a square of dough with a little of the beaten egg. Place a little tuna mixture in the centre of the dough, then fold it in half in a triangular shape. Pinch the edges together well to firmly seal in the filling. Repeat with the remainder of the rolled dough, then do the same with the second half.

Bring a large saucepan of salted water to the boil. Add the triangles and bring the water back to the boil. Do not let the water boil too rapidly or the pasta may burst: keep it just boiling steadily. Cook for 4–5 minutes, then drain well.

Serve the triangles with one of the sauces and offer Parmesan cheese at the table.

SPAGHETTI WITH CREAM, PRAWNS AND BRANDY

Serves 6

This dish is quick-baked in the oven, which really enhances the rich flavours of the cream, prawns and brandy.

INGREDIENTS

450 g/1 lb fresh spaghetti

salt to taste

150 g/6 oz double cream

2 tbsp finely chopped fresh parsley

4 tbsp brandy or cognac

450 g/1 lb shelled uncooked prawns (substitute cooked if necessary)

freshly ground black pepper

Preheat the oven to 190°C/ 375°F/Gas Mark 5. As the pasta is cooking, bring the cream to the boiling point in a saucepan. Add the chopped fresh parsley to the cream, together with the brandy or cognac. Remove the cream from the heat and let it stand so that the flavours infuse.

Finely chop the prawns. If they are uncooked, add them to the cream and return it to the heat until it re-boils. There is no need to bring cooked prawns to the boil.

Spread out on a baking sheet a sheet of aluminium foil large enough to fold over and completely envelop both pasta and sauce. Place the drained pasta in the middle of the foil and pour the sauce on top. Lift the edges of the foil upwards around the pasta and fold them together, completely sealing the prawn mixture.

Bake in the oven for about 5 minutes, then transfer the foil package to a serving dish. Unseal at the table, sprinkle with black pepper and serve.

Farfalle with Salmon

Serves 4–6

This is a recipe you can fall back on when you have friends to visit. It works equally well either as an appetizer or as a main meal if served with plenty of crusty bread and salad.

INGREDIENTS

150 g/6 oz broccoli florets

4 tbsp butter

225 g/8 oz thinly sliced leeks

4 plum tomatoes, peeled, seeded and chopped

60 g/2½ oz double cream for whipping

225 g/8 oz smoked salmon, cut into strips

450 g/1 lb fresh farfalle

ground black pepper

Divide the broccoli into tiny florets, then blanch in boiling water for 2 minutes. Drain and refresh in cold water. Reserve.

Melt the butter in a pan and sauté the sliced leeks for 4 minutes, stirring frequently. Add the drained broccoli and tomatoes, double cream and smoked salmon and heat through, stirring occasionally. Cover with a lid and reserve.

Meanwhile, cook the farfalle in plenty of salted boiling water for 1–2 minutes or until 'al dente'. Drain and return to the pan. Add the cream and smoked salmon mixture. Toss lightly and serve immediately sprinkled with freshly ground black pepper.

Chicken and Tarragon Sauce

Serves 4

This is a simple sauce which goes well with any pasta. It may also be layered with lasagne, noodles or shapes in baked dishes. Turkey may be used instead of chicken.

INGREDIENTS

2–4 tbsp butter

1 small onion, finely chopped

1 bay leaf

75 g/3 oz button mushrooms, sliced

75 g/3 oz plain flour

300 ml/½ pint chicken stock

175 ml/6 fl oz milk

225–350 g/8–12 oz boneless, skinned, cooked chicken, diced

2 tbsp chopped tarragon

salt and freshly ground black pepper

125 g/5 oz single cream

Melt 2 tablespoons of the butter in a saucepan. Add the onion and bay leaf and cook, stirring occasionally, for 15 minutes or until the onion is softened slightly but not browned. Add the mushrooms and continue to cook for 10–15 minutes, until they give up their juice and this evaporates completely, leaving the reduced vegetables and the butter.

Stir in the flour, then gradually pour in the stock and bring to the boil, stirring all the time. Stir in the milk, bring back to the boil, then add the chicken and tarragon with seasoning to taste. Reduce the heat, cover the pan and simmer gently for 10 minutes. Stir in the cream and heat gently without boiling. If you like, beat in the remaining butter to enrich the sauce and make it rather special.

Duck and Orange Dressing

Serves 4

A rich dressing for narrow noodles or spaghetti, and a good way of making a couple of large duck breasts serve four. Make a salad of grated courgette and carrot as an accompaniment.

INGREDIENTS

2 large boneless duck breasts, skinned and cut into fine strips

1 tbsp plain flour

salt and freshly ground black pepper

½ tsp ground mace

zest and juice of 1 orange

1 tbsp oil

1 onion, halved and thinly sliced

225 g/9 oz button mushrooms, sliced

300 ml/½ pint dry red wine

4 tbsp redcurrant jelly

Place the strips of duck meat in a bowl or plastic bag. Add the flour, plenty of seasoning, the mace and orange zest. Mix well, or close and shake the bag.

Heat the oil in a large frying pan. Add the duck and brown the strips all over, then add the onion and cook, stirring often, for about 15 minutes or until the onion is softened slightly but not browned. Stir in the mushrooms and cook for 10 minutes or so, until they are well reduced. Pour in the orange juice and wine, then bring to the boil. Add the redcurrant jelly and boil for about 1 minute, stirring.

Taste for seasoning, then ladle the duck sauce over freshly cooked, drained pasta and serve at once.

PORK AND PASTA ROLLS

Serves 4

Pork and cider make a classic combination in these delicious pasta rolls.

INGREDIENTS

150 g/1 lb ground pork

100 g/4 oz fresh white breadcrumbs

1 onion, finely chopped

1 tbsp chopped fresh rosemary

2 tbsp chopped fresh parsley

2 eggs, beaten

salt and freshly ground black pepper

½ quantity Pasta Dough (page 27)

300 ml/½ pint dry cider

600 ml/1 pint chicken stock

3 tbsp butter

2 tbsp plain flour

rosemary sprigs, to garnish (optional)

Mix the ground pork, breadcrumbs, onion, rosemary, parsley and half the beaten egg. Add plenty of seasoning and pound the mixture until all the ingredients are thoroughly combined.

Roll out the dough into a rectangle measuring slightly larger than 43 cm/ 17 in × 25 cm/10 in. Trim the edges, then brush the pasta with beaten egg. Spread the meat mixture all over the roll, leaving a narrow border around the edge. Roll up the pasta from the long end. Seal the end of the roll with more beaten egg and press it down on the roll with a blunt knife.

Set the oven at 180°C/350°F/Gas Mark 4. Prepare a large saucepan of boiling water. Cut the roll in half or quarters, depending on the size of the saucepan. Carefully lower the pieces of roll into the water and simmer for 3 minutes. Wrapping a couple of bands of folded foil around the roll helps with lowering it into the water and lifting it out again; otherwise use a large fish slice and slotted spoon to drain the pieces of roll. Cut the roll into 16 slices and place them in an oven-proof casserole.

Heat the cider and stock together, then pour them over the rolls, cover and bake for 1 hour. Meanwhile, beat the butter into the flour. Transfer the cooked rolls to a serving dish or individual plates and keep hot. Bring the cooking juices to the boil in a saucepan, then gradually whisk in the butter and flour paste. Boil for 3 minutes, then taste for seasoning. Spoon a little of the sauce over the rolls and offer the rest separately. Garnish with fresh rosemary sprigs if you like.

TURKEY AND LASAGNE RING

Serves 4

Fill the middle of this ring with vegetables, such as sautéed courgette, glazed carrots or green beans sautéed with red peppers and onions.

INGREDIENTS

100 g/4 oz spinach-flavoured pasta

100 g/4 oz Pasta Dough (page 27)

2 tbsp oil

450 g/1 lb leeks, chopped

300 g/12 oz diced turkey

1 cooking apple, peeled, cored and chopped

100 g/4 oz fresh breadcrumbs

2 tbsp chopped sage

salt and freshly ground black pepper

1 egg

Mushroom Sauce (page 43) to serve

Roll out both doughs separately and cut them into wide bands, or lasagne, long enough to line a 900 ml-ring pan. Cook the lasagne in boiling salted water for 3 minutes, then drain, and rinse under cold water. Lay out on double-thick kitchen paper.

Heat the oil in a large saucepan. Add the leeks and cook for about 15 minutes, until they are greatly reduced in volume and softened. Remove from the heat. Mix in the turkey, apple, breadcrumbs, sage, plenty of seasoning and egg. Make sure the ingredients are thoroughly combined.

Set the oven at 180°C/350°F/Gas Mark 4. Grease a 900 ml-ring pan. Line it with lasagne, alternating the verde and plain sheets, and leaving the pasta overlapping the rim of the pan. Fill with the turkey mixture, then fold the ends of the lasagne over neatly. Cover with greased foil and bake for 1 hour. Check that the turkey mixture is cooked through by inserting the point of a knife into the middle of it and taking out a small portion.

Invert the ring on a platter. Cut into slices to serve and offer mushroom sauce.

Lamb and Pasta Hotpot

Serves 4

This is a heart-warming winter stew! Beef, pork or bacon may all be used instead of lamb.
Offer some crusty bread to mop up the juices.

INGREDIENTS

1 tbsp oil

550 g/1¼ lb lean, boneless lamb, cubed

1 onion, chopped

2 carrots, diced

2 rosemary sprigs

salt and freshly ground black pepper

600 ml/1 pint light beer

600 ml/1 pint water

260 g/9 oz frozen peas

450 g/1 lb fresh fusilli

125 g/5 oz soured cream

paprika

croûtons, to serve

Heat the oil in a large flame-proof casserole or heavy-based saucepan. Add the lamb and brown the cubes all over. Stir in the onion, carrots, rosemary sprigs and seasoning. Cook, stirring, for a few minutes, then add the beer and water. Bring just to the boil, reduce the heat and cover the pan. Leave the hotpot to simmer for 1¼ hours, stirring occasionally until the lamb is tender and the cooking liquor is well flavoured.

Taste for seasoning, then add the peas. Bring back to the boil, reduce the heat and cover the pot. Simmer for 15 minutes. Add the pasta, stir well, then bring back to the boil. Partially cover the pan and cook for 5 minutes, only allowing the hotpot to boil very slowly.

Top individual portions of the hotpot with soured cream and sprinkle with paprika. Sprinkle with croûtons and serve piping hot.

Venison on a Bed of Pasta

Serves 6

Venison is delicious in this lightly spiced, creamy sauce. For a cheaper alternative, prepare a braising piece of beef such as chuck, in the same way. Ask the butcher to truss the meat neatly so that it stays in good shape during cooking. Serve with green beans and glazed carrot strips.

INGREDIENTS

1.5 kg/3 lb boneless leg of venison
1 onion, thinly sliced
1 carrot, diced
1 tbsp coriander seeds, coarsely crushed
1 tsp green peppercorns, crushed
1 bay leaf
1 bottle dry white wine
2 tbsp pistachio oil
2 tbsp oil
75 g/3 oz diced smoked bacon
salt and freshly ground black pepper
75 g/3 oz roughly chopped prunes
100 g/4 oz crimini mushrooms, sliced
3 tbsp butter
25 g/1 oz plain flour
450 g/1 lb fresh noodles
575 ml/20 fl oz soured cream

Place the venison in a mixing bowl. Add the onion, carrot, coriander seeds, peppercorns and bay leaf. Pour the white wine over the meat, then gently trickle the pistachio oil over. Cover and leave to marinate in the refrigerator for 24 hours, turning the meat in the marinade as often as possible.

Heat the oil in a large flame-proof casserole or heavy-based saucepan. Brown the piece of venison very well on all sides. Add the bacon, cook for 2–3 minutes, then add all the marinade. Add plenty of seasoning and pour in enough water to cover two-thirds of the venison. Bring just to the boil, reduce the heat and cover with a close-fitting lid. Simmer for 1½ hours, then carefully turn the venison. Add the prunes and mushrooms and cook for a further 1¼ hours. Cream the butter and flour to a smooth paste and set aside.

Add the noodles to the pan. Bring back to the boil, then reduce the heat and simmer for a further 10 minutes. Lift the venison from the pan. Use a slotted spoon to transfer the noodles to a heated serving dish. Cover and keep hot. Boil the cooking liquid rapidly in the open pan until it is reduced to about 425 ml/¾ pint.

Meanwhile, carve the venison and arrange it on top of the noodles. Cover and keep hot. Whisk the flour paste into the sauce and boil for 2 minutes, whisking all the time. Remove from the heat, stir in the soured cream and taste for seasoning. Heat gently if necessary but do not boil. Pour some of the sauce over the meat and noodles and offer the rest separately.

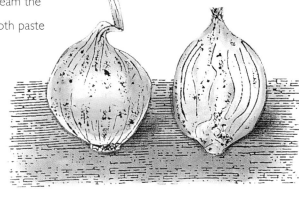

PASTA WITH HAM AND TWO PEPPERS

Serves 4

Most of the ingredients in this recipe can be found in any pantry.

INGREDIENTS

2 tbsp dried red peppercorns, coarsely crushed

2 tbsp dried green peppercorns, coarsely crushed

4 tbsp chopped fresh parsley

4 tbsp snipped chives

½ cucumber, peeled

2 tsp chopped mint (optional)

450 g/1 lb fresh pasta

50 g/2 oz butter

300 g/12 oz lean cooked ham, finely shredded

Mix the red and green peppercorns, chopped parsley and snipped chives. Cut the cucumber into 2.5 cm/1 in lengths, then slice these pieces vertically and cut the slices into fine strips. Mix the mint into the cucumber strips.

While the pasta is cooking, melt the butter. Toss the hot butter and the ham into the drained pasta. Sprinkle the peppercorn mixture over and toss lightly. Top each portion with shredded cucumber and serve at once.

MALTAGLIATI WITH LAMB AND CHIVES

Serves 4

If preferred you can use ground lamb, but it is preferable to buy leg of lamb and chop the meat very finely.

INGREDIENTS

3 tbsp olive oil

2 garlic cloves, peeled and finely chopped

1 large onion, peeled and chopped

250 g/10 oz lean lamb, trimmed and finely chopped

400 g/14 oz tin chopped tomatoes

1 tbsp tomato purée

4 tbsp red wine

1 tbsp snipped fresh chives

salt and ground black pepper

450 g/1 lb fresh maltagliati

2–3 tbsp freshly grated Parmesan cheese

extra snipped fresh chives

Heat the olive oil in a pan and sauté the garlic and onion for 5 minutes or until softened. Add the chopped lamb and continue to sauté for 5 minutes, stirring frequently until browned.

Add the chopped tomatoes, the tomato purée blended with 2 tablespoons water, and the red wine. Bring to the boil, reduce the heat, cover with a lid and simmer for 40 minutes or until a thick sauce is formed. Add the snipped chives and seasoning to taste, and continue to simmer for 5 minutes while cooking the pasta.

Cook the pasta in plenty of salted boiling water for 1–2 minutes or until 'al dente'. Drain and return to the pan. Add the meat sauce, toss lightly, then serve sprinkled with the grated Parmesan cheese and extra snipped fresh chives.

STEAK SAUCE WITH SALSA

Serves 4

A really simple steak sauce, this one, with some onion and mushrooms to complement the flavour of the meat. The taste-bud awakener is the salsa – a Mexican-style cold sauce of tomato, onion and chilli. Serve it in a separate dish so that it can be spooned over the beef and pasta to taste. Noodles or spaghetti are the ideal pasta for this.

INGREDIENTS

75 g/3 oz ripe tomatoes, peeled

1 red onion, finely chopped

2 fresh green chillies, seeded and chopped

1 garlic clove, crushed

salt and freshly ground black pepper

1 tsp caster sugar

zest and juice of ½ lime

3 tbsp chopped fresh coriander

675 g/1½ lb lean sirloin steak, sliced across the grain and cut into strips

3 tbsp all-purpose flour

large knob of beef dripping or 2 tbsp oil

1 large onion, halved and thinly sliced

1 bay leaf

2 parsley sprigs

2 thyme sprigs

225 g/9 oz button mushrooms, sliced

good beef stock or tinned consommé

dash of Worcestershire sauce

Make the salsa first but not too far in advance of serving. Halve the tomatoes, discard the cores leading from the stems, then chop them. Mix with the onion, chillies and garlic. Add plenty of seasoning, the sugar, lime zest and juice and the coriander. Mix well. Taste to check the seasoning and set aside.

Toss the steak with the flour and plenty of seasoning. Melt the beef dripping or heat the oil in a large frying pan. When the fat is shimmering hot, add the steak and stir-fry the strips until they are browned. If the fat is hot enough, and particularly if using dripping, the strips will seal, brown and cook quickly. Add the sliced onion and herbs, reduce the heat and cook for 15 minutes, or until the onion is softened slightly. Stir in the sliced mushrooms and cook for a further 15 minutes.

Pour in the stock and add Worcestershire sauce to taste. Bring to the boil, stirring, reduce the heat and simmer gently for 5 minutes. Taste for seasoning and remove the herb sprigs before serving with freshly cooked, drained pasta.

PORK WITH DATES AND GINGER

Serves 4

Serve this sweet and slightly spicy dish with plain fine noodles or tagliatelle and a fresh onion salad.

INGREDIENTS

2 tbsp oil

50 g/2 oz peeled chopped fresh root ginger

1 cinnamon stick

675 g/1½ lb lean boneless pork, diced

salt and freshly ground black pepper

100 g/4 oz fresh dates

180 ml/6½ fl oz fresh orange juice

180 ml/6½ fl oz water

125 g/5 oz soured cream

Heat the oil in a frying pan and add the root ginger, cinnamon and pork. Sprinkle in plenty of seasoning, then cook, stirring occasionally, until the pork is lightly browned and cooked through.

Meanwhile, slit the dates and remove their stones, then rub off their papery skins and slice the fruit. Add the orange juice and water to the pork. Bring to the boil, reduce the heat and simmer hard for 10 minutes. Stir in the dates, simmer for 5 minutes and taste for seasoning.

Remove the pan from the heat, swirl in the soured cream and serve at once, ladled over individual portions of freshly cooked, drained pasta.

JALAPEÑO BEEF AND YAM

Serves 4

Here is a recipe to transform old-fashioned stewed beef into a multinational meal!
Of course, a regular beef stew tastes really good with pasta but this is a bit different, and the combination of yams
and bell peppers makes the beef go a lot further.

INGREDIENTS

450 g/1 lb lean chuck steak, diced
quite small

2 tbsp plain flour

salt and freshly ground black pepper

2 tbsp oil or knob of beef dripping

2 onions, chopped

600 ml/1 pint water

675 g/1½ lb yam, peeled and cut into
2.5 cm/1 in cubes

2 garlic cloves, crushed

1 red pepper, seeded and diced

1 green pepper, seeded and diced

100 g/4 oz can jalapeño chillies,
drained and chopped

2 tbsp currants

zest and juice of 1 lime

2 tbsp chopped fresh coriander

2 tsp thyme leaves

Set the oven at 180°C/350°F/ Gas Mark 4. Coat the meat with flour and plenty of salt. Add a little pepper. Heat half the oil or dripping in a flame-proof casserole. Add the meat and brown the pieces all over, then add half the chopped onion and cook for a few minutes. Pour in the water and bring to the boil. Cover the casserole tightly and transfer it to the oven. Cook for 1 hour, then reduce the heat to 170°C/325°F/Gas Mark 3, and cook for a further 2 hours, or until the meat is very tender. Stir occasionally, scraping the side of the casserole to remove any residue which bakes on above the line of the stew.

Meanwhile, cook the yam in boiling water for 10 minutes, or until just tender. Drain. Heat the remaining oil or dripping and add the rest of the onion with the garlic, red and green peppers, chillies and currants. Cook over medium heat, stirring often, for 20 minutes, until the onion and peppers are well cooked. Stir in the lime zest and juice and herbs. Add the yam and mix well. Remove from the heat, cover and set aside until the beef is cooked. It is a good idea to prepare the yam mixture immediately after the steak, so that the flavours have time to mingle and develop.

Stir the yam mixture into the stew and reheat thoroughly on the hob before serving. Ladle the sauce over bowls of freshly cooked, drained

SPAGHETTI WITH SMOKED SAUSAGE AND CARROTS

Serves 4

A good, inexpensive and satisfying supper dish: the sweetness of the carrot complements the flavoursome sausage. Try to find smoked sausage made with fresh garlic.

INGREDIENTS

3 tbsp olive oil

I onion, halved and thinly sliced

2 cups coarsely grated carrots

450 g/I lb smoked sausage, cut into strips

salt and freshly ground black pepper

50 g/2 oz butter

450 g/I lb fresh spaghetti

Heat the oil in a large frying pan. Add the onion and cook for 5 minutes, then add the carrots and sausage. Cook, stirring often, for about 10 minutes, until the pieces of sausage are browned in parts and the carrots are lightly cooked. Add seasoning to taste. Add the butter to the carrot and sausage mixture, toss into the freshly cooked, drained spaghetti and serve.

RICH MEAT RAGÔUT

Serves 4

This is a good Bolognese-style sauce for spooning over pasta or layering with it.

INGREDIENTS

3 tbsp olive oil

I large onion, chopped

2 celery stalks, finely diced

2 carrots, finely diced

I green pepper, seeded and diced

2 garlic cloves, crushed

100 g/4 oz rindless smoked bacon, diced

2 tsp dried marjoram

I thyme sprig

I bay leaf

100 g/4 oz lean minced pork

100 g/4 oz lean minced braising steak

salt and freshly ground black pepper

I tbsp plain flour

I tbsp tomato purée

2 × 400 g/14 oz tins chopped tomatoes

300 ml/½ pint dry red wine

4 tbsp chopped fresh parsley

fresh grated Parmesan cheese, to

Heat the oil in a large, heavy saucepan. Add the onion, celery, carrots, green pepper, garlic, bacon, marjoram, thyme and bay leaf. Cook, stirring, until the onion is slightly softened and the bacon cooked – about 15 minutes.

Add the pork and steak, and continue to cook, stirring, for 10 minutes. Stir in seasoning, flour and tomato purée, tomatoes and wine, then bring the sauce to the boil. Reduce the heat, cover and simmer the sauce for 1½ hours, stirring occasionally. Taste and adjust the seasoning before mixing in the parsley. Serve over freshly cooked pasta with Parmesan cheese.

Spaghetti with Smoked Sausage and Carrots ▶

PASTA CARBONARA

Serves 4

With just a few simple ingredients, this classic dish can be served in minutes.

INGREDIENTS

50 g/2 oz butter

300 g/12 oz cooked ham, shredded

8 eggs

salt and freshly ground black pepper

150 ml/¼ pint single cream

450 g/1 lb fresh tagliatelle

plenty of chopped fresh parsley

freshly grated Parmesan cheese, to serve

Melt the butter in a large, heavy bottomed or non stick saucepan. Add the ham and cook for 2 minutes. Beat the eggs with seasoning and cream. Reduce the heat under the pan, if necessary, then pour in the eggs and cook them gently, stirring all the time until they are creamy. Do not cook the eggs until they set and scramble, and do not increase the heat to speed up the process or the carbonara will be spoiled.

The pasta should be added to the boiling water at the same time as adding the eggs to the pan. This way, the pasta will be drained and hot, ready to be tipped into the eggs. When the eggs are half set, add the pasta, mix well until the eggs are creamy and serve at once, sprinkled with parsley. Offer the freshly grated Parmesan cheese separately.

PENNE WITH BACON, TOMATO AND ROSEMARY

Serves 6

Penne are traditionally used in this well-known recipe. Be sure to use fresh rosemary for the best flavour.

INGREDIENTS

2 tbsp olive oil

3 garlic cloves

1 medium onion

100 g/¼ lb bacon or *pancetta*, roughly chopped

900 g/2 lb fresh or canned plum tomatoes

1 tsp sugar

2 tsp finely chopped fresh rosemary

450 g/1 lb fresh penne

salt to taste

Heat the oil in a frying pan and cook the garlic and onion to soften. Add the bacon and cook gently for 2–3 minutes. Stir in the tomatoes and sugar. Simmer the sauce for 15–20 minutes. Add the rosemary 5 minutes before serving. Season and serve over the freshly cooked, drained penne.

Pasta Carbonara ▶

HAY AND STRAW WITH CREAM AND PARMA HAM

Serves 4

Noodles are now available in a variety of flavours including sun-dried tomato and squid. Vary the colours of this dish with a combination of noodles to make it look really attractive.

INGREDIENTS

300 ml/½ pint double cream

1 tbsp finely chopped fresh sage

1 tbsp finely chopped fresh parsley

150 ml/¼ pint dry white wine

100 g/4 oz Parma ham

225 g/½ lb plain fresh noodles

225 g/½ lb fresh spinach noodles

2 tbsp butter

Bring the cream to the boil, add the sage, parsley and white wine. Keep boiling to reduce the volume of liquid by one third. When reduced, dice the ham and add it to the cream. Remove from the heat.

Drain the pasta and whisk in the butter. Toss it in the mixture and serve very hot.

TAGLIATELLE NESTS

Serves 4

These make a good first course or light lunch.

INGREDIENTS

300 g/12 oz fresh tagliatelle verde

2 tomatoes, peeled, seeded and diced

2 tbsp walnut oil

3 tbsp sunflower oil

juice of 1 lime

salt and freshly ground black pepper

1 tbsp chopped fresh mint

225 g/½ lb rinded bacon slices

100 g/¼ lb shelled fresh peas

4 small courgette

4 tbsp soured cream

mint sprigs, to garnish (optional)

Cook the tagliatelle in boiling salted water for 3 minutes, then drain well, and turn into a bowl. Add the tomatoes, both types of oil, the lime juice, seasoning and the mint. Toss well, cover and leave to cool.

Grill the bacon slices until they are crisp, turning once. Drain them on absorbent kitchen paper and leave to cool. Cook the peas in boiling water for 15 minutes, then drain and set aside. Trim the courgette, peel them very thinly so that they are a bright green outside, then halve them lengthwise. Slice the courgette thinly and mix them with the peas.

Divide the tagliatelle and its dressing between four plates, swirling it into nests. Top the nests with the courgette and pea mixture. Crush the crisply grilled bacon and sprinkle it over the courgette and pea mixture, then top with a little soured cream. Mint sprigs may be added as a garnish, if liked.

Timbales, Moulds and Bakes

SALMON AND PASTA TIMBALES

Serves 4

Ideal for a light supper or an appetizer. Add ground turmeric to the flour, when making up the pasta dough, for an unusual spicy taste.

INGREDIENTS

50 g/2 oz Pasta Dough (see page 27) flavoured with 1 tsp ground turmeric

salt and freshly ground black pepper

175 g/7 oz tin salmon

100 g/4 oz fresh white breadcrumbs

1 tbsp finely chopped scallions

3 basil sprigs, finely shredded, or 1 tbsp fresh parsley

50 g/2 oz ricotta cheese, strained

1 egg, separated

basil or parsley sprigs and halved lemon slices, to garnish

Roll out the pasta very thinly. Take a ramekin dish and cut a paper pattern of the base. Grease and base-line 4 ramekins with non-stick bakers' parchment. Cut 12 circles of pasta, then cook them in boiling salted water for 3 minutes. Drain the circles and place a circle of pasta in the bottom of each ramekin. Lay the remaining pasta out on absorbent kitchen paper. Set the oven at 180°C/350°F/Gas Mark 4.

Drain the salmon, remove any skin and bone, then mash it. Mix with the breadcrumbs, scallions, basil or parsley and ricotta cheese. Add seasoning and beat in the egg yolk. Whisk the egg white until stiff, then fold it into the salmon mixture. Divide the mixture roughly in half, then spoon one portion into the dishes, dividing it equally between them and spreading it neatly. Top each with a circle of pasta, then divide the remaining mixture between the dishes. Finally, top each with a circle of pasta. Stand on a baking sheet and cover with foil. Bake for 25–30 minutes, or until the salmon mixture is set. It will also have risen.

Allow to stand for 2 minutes, then slide a knife around the inside of each ramekin. Invert the timbales on individual plates. Remove the non-stick bakers' parchment. Serve garnished with basil or parsley and lemon.

Seafood Lasagne

Serves 6

This is one of my favourite pasta dishes.

INGREDIENTS

300 g/12 oz spinach-flavoured pasta dough or fresh lasagne verde

2 tbsp olive oil

2 tbsp butter

1 onion, finely chopped

1 bay leaf

40 g/1½ oz plain flour

300 ml/½ pint dry white wine

300 ml/½ pint fish stock

75 g/3 oz button mushrooms, sliced

salt and freshly ground black pepper

675 g/1½ lb white-fish fillet, skinned and cut into chunks

225 g/8 oz peeled cooked prawns, thawed if frozen

450 g/1 lb mussels, cooked and shelled (discard any that are shut after cooking)

2 tbsp chopped fresh parsley

1 quantity Béchamel Sauce (page 43)

50 g/2 oz grated Cheddar cheese

Cut the rolled-out pasta into large squares (about 7.5 cm/5 in) or rectangular sheets. Lower the pieces of pasta one at a time into a large saucepan of boiling salted water. Bring back to the boil and cook for 3 minutes. Drain and rinse under cold water. Lay the pasta on double-thick absorbent kitchen paper.

Set the oven at 180°C/350°F/Gas Mark 4. Heat the oil and butter in a saucepan and add the onion and bay leaf. Cook for 10 minutes, until the onion is softened slightly, then stir in the flour. Slowly pour in the wine and stock and bring to the boil, stirring all the time. Add the mushrooms and seasoning, then simmer for 10 minutes. Remove from the heat before stirring in the fish, prawns, mussels and parsley. Layer this fish sauce and the lasagne in a large oven-proof dish, ending with a layer of lasagne. Pour the béchamel sauce evenly over the pasta, then sprinkle the cheese on top. Bake for 40–50 minutes, until golden-brown and bubbling hot.

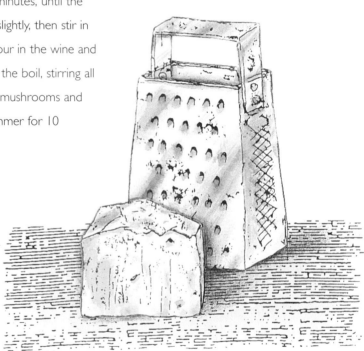

TAGLIATELLE TURKEY BAKE

Serves 4–6

A delicious way of using up leftovers from a roast turkey dinner.

INGREDIENTS

2 tbsp olive oil

1 onion, chopped

1 garlic clove, crushed

1 green pepper, seeded and diced

1 tsp dried marjoram

250 g/9 oz diced cooked turkey

mushrooms, thinly sliced

400 g/14 oz tin chopped tomatoes

3 tbsp chopped fresh parsley

salt and freshly ground black pepper

450 g/1 lb fresh tagliatelle, cooked

4 fresh basil sprigs

600 ml/1 pint Béchamel Sauce (page 43)

100 g/4 oz mozzarella cheese, diced

2 tbsp freshly grated Parmesan cheese

Set the oven at 200°C/400°F/Gas Mark 6. Heat the oil in a large saucepan. Add the onion, garlic, green pepper and marjoram. Cook, stirring often, for 15–20 minutes, until the onion is softened. Stir in the turkey, mushrooms, tomatoes, parsley and seasoning. Remove from the heat and mix in the tagliatelle. Spoon the mixture into an oven-proof dish and press the top down with the back of a metal spoon so the noodles are fairly flat.

Use scissors to shred the basil and soft stems into the béchamel sauce. Taste for seasoning, then pour the sauce evenly over the pasta mixture. Mix the mozzarella and Parmesan, then sprinkle this over the sauce. Bake for 40–45 minutes, until browned.

ASPARAGUS ROULADES

Serves 4

Halve the quantities if you want to serve these as a light first course.

INGREDIENTS

½ quantity Pasta Dough (page 27)

butter for greasing

100 g/4 oz cream cheese

4 tbsp freshly grated Parmesan cheese

2 tbsp snipped chives

50 g/2 oz fresh breadcrumbs

salt and freshly ground black pepper

32 fine asparagus stalks, lightly steamed

I quantity Béchamel Sauce (page 43)

Roll out the pasta into a long sheet, slightly larger than 25 × 51 cm/10 × 20 in. (If it is more practical, roll out the dough in two batches.) Trim the dough neatly, cut it in half lengthwise, then across at eight equal intervals. This will make 16 rectangles measuring 12.5 × 6 cm/ 5 × 2½ in. Cook these in boiling salted water for 3 minutes. Drain, rinse in cold water and lay out on double-thick absorbent kitchen paper.

Set the oven at 200°C/400°F/Gas Mark 6. Butter an oven-proof dish. Mix the cream cheese, half the Parmesan, the chives and breadcrumbs. Add a little seasoning. Spread or dot a little of the cheese mixture over a piece of pasta, then lay a couple of asparagus stalks on top and roll the pasta over to enclose them. Lay in the dish with the join in the pasta downward. Fill all the pasta in the same way.

Pour the béchamel sauce over the pasta and sprinkle with the remaining Parmesan. Bake for 20–25 minutes, until bubbling hot and lightly browned.

SPICED SQUASH AND PASTA BAKE

Serves 4

This is also a good recipe for pumpkin. Buy only good-quality curry powder prepared by a reputable manufacturer as the cheaper unknown brands can be unpleasant.

INGREDIENTS

2 tbsp butter

1 onion, chopped

1 garlic clove, crushed

675 g/1½ lb summer squash, seeded, peeled, and cut in small cubes

1 tsp mild curry powder

150 g/6 oz button mushrooms, sliced

25 g/1 oz ground almonds

1 tbsp all-purpose flour

300 ml/½ pint coconut milk

zest of 1 lime

salt and freshly ground black pepper

300 g/12 oz fresh fusilli, cooked

300 ml/½ pint single cream

flaked almonds

Set the oven at 180°C/350°F/Gas Mark 4. Melt the butter in a large saucepan. Add the onion and garlic and cook for 5 minutes, then stir in the squash, curry powder and mushrooms. Cook for 25–30 minutes, stirring often, until the squash is tender. Stir in the ground almonds and flour, then pour in the coconut milk, stirring all the time, and bring to the simmering point. Remove from the heat and add the lime zest with seasoning to taste.

Mix the pasta with the cream and turn half of it into an oven-proof dish or casserole. Spread the pasta out in an even layer, top with the squash mixture, then cover with the remaining pasta in an even layer. Sprinkle the almonds over the top. Bake for 30 minutes, until lightly browned on top.

CAULIFLOWER AND STILTON TERRINE

Serves 6

Serve this terrine in thick slices, accompanied by a tomato sauce, for a light appetizer.

INGREDIENTS

450 g/1 lb cauliflower

150 g/6 oz blue Stilton cheese, finely crumbled

225 g/8 oz fresh white breadcrumbs

8 spring onions, finely chopped

1 tbsp chopped fresh sage

425 ml/15 fl oz soured cream

4 tbsp dry sherry

2 eggs

salt and freshly ground black pepper

freshly grated nutmeg

butter for greasing

½ quantity spinach-flavoured Pasta Dough or fresh lasagne verde

Good Tomato Sauce (page 40), to serve

Cook the cauliflower in boiling water for 5 minutes, then drain well before chopping the florets. Mix the cauliflower, Stilton, breadcrumbs, spring onions, sage, soured cream, sherry and eggs. Add seasoning and a little nutmeg.

Set the oven at 180°C/350°F/Gas Mark 4. Prepare a bain marie and butter a 900 gramme loaf pan. Cut the fresh pasta into wide strips that are long enough to line the pan widthwise and overhang the sides. Cook the pasta for 3 minutes, drain and rinse in cold water, then lay out to dry on absorbent kitchen paper.

Line the pan completely with bands of pasta, overlapping them neatly. If bought fresh lasagne is not long enough, then overlap strips as you do need some pasta overhanging the rim of the pan. Spread a layer of cauliflower mixture in the base of the pan, then cover with a layer of pasta, cutting it to fit neatly and overlapping pieces as necessary. Continue layering the cauliflower mixture and pasta sheets until the pan is full, ending with the cauliflower mixture.

Fold the ends of the pasta over. Add a final layer of pasta to cover the top of the terrine neatly. Generously butter a piece of greaseproof paper and lay it on top of the pasta. Cover with aluminium foil, sealing it well around the edges of the pan. Stand the pan in the bain marie. Bake for 1½ hours, until the mixture is firm to the touch and cooked through. Allow to stand for 5 minutes after cooking.

Slide a metal fishslice between the pasta and the pan, then invert the terrine on a flat platter. Use a serrated knife to cut the terrine into thick slices and serve with tomato sauce.

NUTTY MUSHROOM BAKE

Serves 4

Most types of pasta work well for the topping of this dish; try spaghetti or tagliatelle instead of penne.

INGREDIENTS

225 g/8 oz dried penne

dash of olive oil, plus 2 tbsp oil

2 tbsp butter

1 onion, chopped

1 garlic clove, crushed

2 tsp dried oregano

150 g/6 oz mushrooms, sliced

400 g/14 oz tin chopped tomatoes

1 heaped tbsp tomato purée

pimiento-stuffed green olives, sliced

75 g/3 oz roasted cashews

salt and freshly ground black pepper

150 g/6 oz grated mature Cheddar cheese

Bring a large saucepan of water to the boil, and add the penne with a dash of olive oil. Cook for about 10 minutes, stirring occasionally, until tender. Drain, return to the saucepan, and stir in the butter until melted. Set aside, covered.

Preheat the oven to 200°C/400°F/ Gas Mark 6. Heat the remaining olive oil in a large frying pan and sauté the onion, garlic and oregano for 3 minutes or until the onion has softened.

Add the sliced mushrooms and cook for a further 5 minutes, stirring occasionally. Stir in the chopped tomatoes and tomato purée. Cover the frying pan and cook for about 10 minutes, stirring occasionally.

Add the sliced olives and the cashews and season with salt and freshly ground black pepper. Continue to cook for a final 2–3 minutes, then transfer the mixture to a shallow, oven-proof dish. Spoon the buttered pasta on top, and sprinkle with the cheese. Bake in the pre-heated oven for 20 minutes, or until the top is crisp and golden.

TOMATO PASTA TIMBALES

Serves 4

An attractive first course, these timbales are very easy to make and are sure to impress your guests.
Make them up to one hour in advance and place them in the oven to bake.

INGREDIENTS

300 g/12 oz dried multicoloured
spaghettini

dash of olive oil, plus extra for greasing

4 small tomato slices

2 tbsp tomato pesto

2 eggs, beaten

60 ml/2½ fl oz milk

salt and freshly ground black pepper

SAUCE

100 g/4 oz sieved tomatoes

1 tbsp sweet soy sauce

4 tbsp chopped fresh basil

salt and freshly ground black pepper

fresh flat parsley sprigs and cherry
tomatoes, to garnish

Bring a large saucepan of water to the boil and add the spaghettini with a dash of olive oil. Cook for about 10 minutes, stirring occasionally, until tender. Drain well.

Preheat the oven to 170°C/325°F/ Gas Mark 3. Grease four ⅓ pint individual oven-proof moulds with a little olive oil and place a circle of waxed paper in the bottom of each. Place a slice of tomato in the base of each mould, then carefully pack in the spaghettini, leaving a 5 mm/¼ in space at the top.

In a small bowl, combine the tomato pesto, eggs, milk and salt and freshly ground black pepper. Beat well then pour into each spaghettini mould, covering the pasta.

Arrange the moulds in a roasting tin with enough boiling water to come halfway up the sides. Bake for about 40 minutes, or until set and firm to the touch.

Meanwhile, to make the sauce, place all the ingredients in a saucepan and heat to simmering point. Simmer for 10 minutes, until thickened slightly.

Run a sharp knife around the edges of each timbale, then invert each onto individual plates. Pour a little sauce around each timbale, and garnish.

PEPPER PASTA SOUFFLÉ

Serves 2

Perfect for a romantic dinner for two. But remember, timing is crucial!
Make sure your guest is seated before removing the soufflé from the oven.

INGREDIENTS

100 g/4 oz fresh spinach tagliatelle

dash of olive oil, plus 2 tbsp oil

1 garlic clove, crushed

225 g/½ lb mixed, coloured peppers,
seeded and cut into thin strips

2 tbsp chopped fresh oregano

SOUFFLE

3 tbsp butter, plus extra for greasing

4 tbsp plain flour

375 ml/13 fl oz milk

40 g/1½ oz freshly grated Parmesan
cheese

4 eggs, separated

Bring a large saucepan of water to the boil and add the fresh spinach tagliatelle with a dash of olive oil. Cook for 3–5 minutes, stirring occasionally, until tender. Drain and roughly chop. Set aside.

Heat the remaining olive oil in a frying pan, and add the garlic. Cook for 1–2 minutes, then stir in the pepper strips with the oregano. Cover and cook over gentle heat for about 10 minutes, stirring occasionally, until the peppers have softened. Remove from the heat and set aside. Preheat the oven to 200°C/400°F/Gas Mark 6.

To make the soufflé, butter two small soufflé dishes and set aside. Melt the butter in a saucepan and stir in the flour to make a paste. Gradually stir in the milk, then bring the sauce to the boil, stirring constantly to prevent lumps, until thickened.

Stir in the Parmesan cheese and heat in the egg yolks, one at a time. Stir in the chopped tagliatelle until evenly coated.

Whisk the egg whites in a clean, dry bowl until stiff. Fold the egg whites into the tagliatelle mixture, then divide between the prepared soufflé dishes. Spoon an equal amount of the pepper mixture on top of each soufflé. Bake for 20–25 minutes until risen and golden. Serve immediately.

CREAMY LEEK AND PASTA FLAN

Serves 6–8

This dish is delicious both fresh out of the oven or served chilled on a hot summer's day with a crisp green salad.

INGREDIENTS

150 g/6 oz dried orecchiette

dash of olive oil, plus 3 tbsp

a little flour, for dredging

300 g/¾ lb puff pastry, thawed if frozen

2 garlic cloves, crushed

450 g/1 lb leeks, washed, trimmed and cut into 2.5 cm/1 in chunks

2 tbsp chopped fresh thyme

2 eggs, beaten

180 ml/6½ fl oz single cream

salt and freshly ground black pepper

125 g/5 oz grated Cheddar cheese

Bring a large saucepan of water to a boil and add the orecchiette with a dash of olive oil. Cook for about 10 minutes, stirring occasionally, until tender. Drain thoroughly and set aside.

Dredge the work surface with a little flour and roll out the pastry. Use to line a greased 25 cm/10 in, loose-bottomed, fluted flan ring. Place in the refrigerator to chill for at least 10 minutes before using.

Preheat the oven to 190°C/375°F/ Gas Mark 5. Heat the remaining olive oil in a large frying pan and sauté the garlic, leeks and thyme for about 5 minutes, stirring occasionally, until tender. Stir in the orecchiette, and continue to cook for a further 2–3 minutes.

Place the beaten eggs in a small bowl then whisk in the cream, salt and freshly ground black pepper.

Transfer the leek and pasta mixture to the pastry shell, spreading out evenly. Pour the egg and cream mixture over the top, then sprinkle with cheese. Bake for 30 minutes until the mixture is firm and the pastry crisp.

LASAGNE BAKED IN THE OVEN

Serves 6

Use either plain lasagne sheets or the spinach variety. Make sure the lasagne is completely covered with sauce otherwise it will dry out during the cooking process.

INGREDIENTS

450 g/1 lb dried lasagne

salt

4 tbsp olive oil

2 garlic cloves, crushed

1 medium onion, sliced

900 g/2 lb fresh or tinned plum tomatoes

1 tsp sugar

2 tbsp fresh basil

600 ml/1 pint Béchamel Sauce

Pre-heat the oven to 220°C/ 425°F/Gas Mark 7. Cook the strips of lasagne until just soft in a large pot of boiling salted water and a little olive oil. Remove from the water, drain them and lay them out, not overlapping, on a lightly greased work surface.

Using a little over half the oil, make a tomato sauce as for Spaghetti Morgan (page 146).

Grease the bottom of a 5 cm/2 in baking dish with the remaining oil.

Cover it with a layer of the cooked pasta. Spoon a layer of the tomato sauce onto the pasta, followed by a layer of the béchamel. Continue with the layers until the dish is full – pasta, sauce, béchamel, pasta, sauce and so on. (Ensure you retain sufficient béchamel for a generous final coating.)

Bake in the pre-heated oven for 15–20 minutes, or until the top has browned well and begun to crisp at the edges.

STUFFED COURGETTE

Serves 4–6

A delicious combination of tender courgettes and fresh coriander mixed with a sweet soy sauce.
You can make the filling and the sauce a day in advance. Re-heat the sauce whilst the courgettes are baking.

INGREDIENTS

100 g/4 oz dried vermicelli, broken into small pieces

dash of olive oil

4 medium courgettes

finely chopped walnuts, to garnish

FILLING

180 ml/6½ oz sweet soy sauce

1 garlic clove, crushed

40 g/1½ oz mushrooms, very finely chopped

3 tbsp chopped fresh coriander

40 g/1½ oz shelled walnuts, very finely chopped

salt and freshly ground black pepper

SAUCE

4 tbsp olive oil

2 garlic cloves, crushed

75 g/3 oz chopped fresh coriander

salt and freshly ground black pepper

3 tbsp vegetable broth

Bring a large saucepan of water to the boil and add the vermicelli with a dash of olive oil. Cook for about 5 minutes, stirring occasionally, until tender. Drain and set aside.

Cut a thin slice lengthwise along the top of each courgette, and chop this piece finely. Using a teaspoon, scoop out the flesh from the middle of the courgette and chop roughly. Arrange the hollowed courgettes in a shallow, oven-proof dish and set aside. Pre-heat the oven to 200°C/400°F/Gas Mark 6.

To make the filling, place the sweet soy sauce and the garlic in a large frying pan and heat gently. Cook for about 1 minute, then stir in the mushrooms. Cook for about 5 minutes, stirring occasionally, then add the coriander. Cook for a further 2–3 minutes, then stir in the chopped walnuts and season to taste with salt and freshly ground black pepper. Simmer for 1–2 minutes, then stir in the cooked vermicelli.

Remove from the heat and, using a teaspoon, stuff the courgettes with the filling, placing any extra around the courgettes in the dish. Cover the dish with foil and bake for 25–30 minutes, until the courgettes are tender.

Meanwhile, to make the sauce, place all the ingredients in a food processor or blender and purée until smooth. Transfer to a small saucepan, and heat gently until warm. Remove the stuffed courgettes from the oven and serve with the coriander sauce, garnished with finely chopped walnuts.

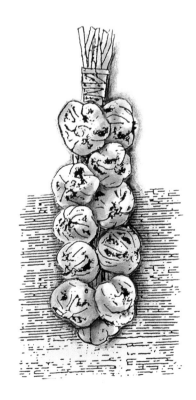

ASPARAGUS RAVIOLI WITH TOMATO SAUCE

Serves 6

A dinner party dish which can be made in advance – the ravioli can even be put in the freezer several weeks before and cooked from frozen. The sauce can be made several hours ahead and re-heated before serving.

INGREDIENTS

⅔ quantity Pasta Dough with 1 tbsp tomato purée beaten into the eggs (page 27)

1 egg, beaten, for brushing

1 quantity Good Tomato Sauce (page 40)

dash of olive oil

chopped fresh herbs, to garnish

FILLING

2 tbsp olive oil

1 garlic clove, crushed

1 onion, very finely chopped

225 g/½ lb fresh asparagus, very finely chopped

salt and freshly ground black pepper

Keep the fresh pasta dough covered with cling film at room temperature, and the tomato sauce in a saucepan, ready to re-heat before serving.

To make the filling, heat the olive oil in a frying pan and sauté the garlic and onion for about 3 minutes, until the onion has softened. Add the chopped fresh asparagus, and season with salt and freshly ground black pepper. Sauté the asparagus mixture for about 10 minutes, until softened. Set aside and allow to cool completely.

To make the ravioli, cut the pasta dough in half. Roll out one half to a rectangle slightly larger than 35.5 × 25 cm/14 × 10 in. Trim the edges of the dough neatly. Cover the rectangle with the plastic wrap to prevent it drying out. Roll out the other half of the dough to the same measurements. Do not trim the edges.

Place half teaspoonfuls of the filling mixture in lines, spaced about 2 cm/¾ in apart, all over the trimmed rectangle of pasta dough. Lightly brush the beaten egg in lines around the filling mixture, to make the square shapes for the ravioli. Lay the other rectangle of pasta dough on top and, starting at one end, seal in the filling by lightly pressing the dough, pushing out any trapped air and gently flattening the filling, making little packages. Using a sharp knife or pastry wheel, cut down and then across in lines around the filling to make the individual square ravioli shapes.

To cook the ravioli, bring a large saucepan of water to the boil and add the ravioli with a dash of olive oil. Cook for about 6 minutes, stirring occasionally, until tender. Drain thoroughly and set aside.

Meanwhile, re-heat the tomato sauce. Serve the ravioli with the tomato sauce, sprinkled with chopped fresh herbs.

SAVOURY SARDINE CANNELLONI

Serves 4

An inexpensive dish for a midweek meal. The sardine and cheese mixture is also good for filling ravioli or tortellini.

INGREDIENTS

½ quantity Pasta Dough (page 27)

2 × 100 g/4 oz tins sardines in oil

1 onion, chopped

1 garlic clove, crushed

150 g/6 oz fresh white breadcrumbs

75 g/3 oz button mushrooms, chopped

100 g/4 oz low-fat soft cheese

100 g/4 oz grated Cheddar cheese

zest and juice of 1 lemon

salt and freshly ground black pepper

butter for greasing

1 quantity Good Tomato Sauce (page 40)

Roll out the pasta into a thin 40 cm/16 in square. Cut it into 10 × 10 cm/4 × 4 in wide strips, then cut the strips across to make 16 squares. Bring a large pan of salted water to the boil, and cook the pieces of pasta, a few at a time if necessary, for 3 minutes. Drain and rinse under cold water, then lay out on double-thick absorbent kitchen paper.

Pour the oil from the sardines into a small saucepan. Add the onion and garlic, then cook, stirring often, for 10 minutes. Remove from the heat. Mash the sardines and add them to the onion and garlic. Mix in the breadcrumbs, mushrooms, soft cheese, three-quarters of the Cheddar cheese, the lemon zest and juice and seasoning to taste.

Set the oven at 200°C/400°F/ Gas Mark 6. Butter an oven proof dish. Place some of the sardine mixture on a piece of pasta, then roll it up into a neat tube and place in the dish with the end of the roll underneath. Repeat with the remaining pasta and filling. Ladle the tomato sauce over the cannelloni, then sprinkle with the remaining cheese. Bake for 25–30 minutes, until the cheese has melted and browned. Serve at once.

PORK AND ROSEMARY RAVIOLI

Serves 12

Depending on where you are in Italy, ravioli may be square or round.

Round filled pasta may also be referred to as agnolotti, again according to regional preferences and traditions.

INGREDIENTS

2 tbsp olive oil

1 onion, finely chopped

2 garlic cloves, crushed

4 juniper berries, crushed

1 tbsp chopped fresh rosemary

½ tsp ground mace

150 g/6 oz lean ground pork

100 g/4 oz fresh white bread crumbs

40 g/1½ oz chopped mushrooms

salt and freshly ground black pepper

2 eggs

1 quantity Pasta Dough (page 27)

TO SERVE

White Wine Sauce (page 42)

75 g/3 oz button mushrooms, thinly sliced

2 tbsp chopped fresh parsley

freshly grated Parmesan cheese

Heat the oil in a saucepan and add the onion, garlic and juniper berries. Cook, stirring, for 15 minutes, or until the onion is softened. Stir in the rosemary, mace, pork, breadcrumbs, mushrooms and plenty of seasoning. Add one egg and thoroughly mix the ingredients, pounding them with the back of the spoon. Beat the remaining egg.

Roll out half the pasta dough slightly larger than a 46-cm/18-in square. Use a 5-cm/2-in round cutter to stamp out circles of pasta, dipping the cutter in flour occasionally so that it cuts the dough cleanly. The best way to do this is to stamp all the circles close together in neat lines in the dough, then lift away the unwanted trimmings when the whole sheet is stamped into circles. You should have about 80 circles. Keep the circles which are not actually being used covered with cling film whilst you fill the ravioli.

Brush a circle of dough with egg, then place some of the meat mixture on it, and cover with a second circle of dough. Pinch the edges of the dough together to seal in the filling. Fill all the ravioli, then roll out the remaining dough and make a second batch.

Cook the ravioli in a large saucepan of boiling water, allowing 15 minutes once the water has come back to the boil. Do this in batches if necessary, then drain the pasta.

Make the sauce but do not add the cream. Add the mushrooms and simmer for 5 minutes before stirring in the cream and parsley. Pour the sauce over the ravioli and serve with Parmesan cheese.

BEEF RAVIOLI WITH TOMATO SAUCE

Serves 6

A traditional Italian favourite.

INGREDIENTS

1 tbsp oil
½ onion, finely chopped
1 garlic clove, crushed
½ tsp dried marjoram
¼ tsp chopped fresh thyme
¼ tsp ground coriander
salt and freshly ground black pepper
50 g/2 oz finely minced sirloin steak
50 g/2 oz minced lean bacon
50 g/2 oz fresh white breadcrumbs
1 egg, beaten
⅔ quantity Pasta Dough (page 27)
1 quantity Good Tomato Sauce (page 40)
freshly grated Parmesan cheese, to serve

Heat the oil in a small saucepan and add the onion, garlic, marjoram, thyme, coriander and seasoning. Cook, stirring, for 5 minutes, then remove from the heat. Mix in the steak, bacon and bread crumbs. Add a little of the egg to bind the ingredients together. Pound the mixture until thoroughly mixed.

Cut the pasta dough in half. Roll out one half into a rectangle measuring slightly larger than 35 × 25 cm/14 × 10 in. Trim the edges of the dough neatly. Cover the rolled-out dough with cling film, then roll out the second portion of dough in the same way but do not bother to trim the edges this time, as a little more dough is needed to cover the stuffing.

Dot small balls of the meat mixture in even lines over the neat rectangle of pasta dough, leaving a gap of 12 cm/¾ in between them. You should have 34–36 ravioli. Whisk a little water into the remaining beaten egg to make it go further if necessary, then brush it over the dough between the mounds of meat. Carefully lay the second sheet of dough over the top. Starting at one end, seal the dough around the meat, carefully pressing out the air and flattening the meat slightly to seal the packages. Use a sharp knife or pastry wheel to trim the pasta edges and cut between the mounds of meat. Make sure the ravioli are neat and flour them slightly if necessary to prevent them sticking together.

Bring a large saucepan of salted water to the boil. Reduce the heat slightly so that it is not bubbling too rapidly and add the ravioli. Keep the water just boiling steadily and cook the ravioli for 10–15 minutes. Meanwhile, heat the tomato sauce. Drain the ravioli, turn them into a serving dish and pour the tomato sauce over them.

Mix lightly before serving with Parmesan cheese.

HARVEST MOONS

Serves 4

These are unusual, filling and nutritious – good if you like spiced food and ideal for a vegetarian lunch.

INGREDIENTS

1 tbsp oil
½ small onion, chopped
½ small carrot, chopped
1 garlic clove, crushed
1 tsp cumin seeds
1 tsp ground coriander
½ × 400 g/14 oz tin chick-peas, drained
1 tomato, peeled and chopped
2 tsp chopped fresh coriander
salt and freshly ground black pepper
½ quantity Pasta Dough (page 27)
1 egg, beaten
2 tbsp lightly salted butter
½ cucumber, peeled and diced
2 tbsp chopped fresh mint

Heat the oil in a small saucepan and add the onion, carrot, garlic, and cumin seeds. Cook, stirring often, for 10 minutes. Stir in the coriander and cook for 2 minutes, then remove the pan from the heat. Roughly mash the chick-peas – they should not be completely smooth. Stir the chick-peas into the onion mixture, then add the tomato, chopped coriander, and seasoning to taste.

Roll out the pasta dough into a 45-cm/18-in square. Use a 5 cm/2 in round cutter to stamp out circles of pasta, dipping the cutter in flour occasionally so that it cuts the dough cleanly. The best way to do this is to stamp all the circles close together in neat lines in the dough, then lift away the unwanted trimmings when the whole sheet is stamped into circles. You should have about 80 circles. Keep the circles which are not actually being used covered with cling film whilst you fill some of them.

Brush a circle of dough with egg, then place some of the chick-pea mixture on it. Fold the pasta in half to make a tiny moon-shaped pastry. Pinch the edges of the dough together to seal in the filling. Repeat with the remaining pasta circles. Cook the pasties in boiling salted water, allowing 3–5 minutes after the water comes back to the boil.

Whilst the pasta is cooking, heat the butter. Add the cucumber and mint and set aside over low heat. Turn the cooked pasta into a warmed serving dish and pour the butter and cucumber mixture over it. Toss well, then serve at once.

THREE-CHEESE CANNELLONI

Serves 4

Only good-quality Parmesan cheese is suitable for the filling in these cannelloni. Bought grated Parmesan, which is strong but lacking the sweetness of a good cheese, will taste too pungent. A fresh, crisp and extremely simple green salad is the perfect accompaniment to complement the richness of the cheese and tomato in the baked dish.

INGREDIENTS

⅓ quantity Pasta Dough (page 27)

225 g/8 oz ricotta cheese

75 g/3 oz freshly grated Parmesan cheese

225 g/8 oz fresh white breadcrumbs

1 tsp dried oregano

1 bunch of watercress, trimmed and chopped

salt and freshly ground black pepper

freshly grated nutmeg

butter for greasing

1 quantity Good Tomato Sauce (page 40)

150 g/6 oz mozzarella cheese, thinly sliced

handful of basil sprigs

Roll out the pasta thinly into a 41 cm/16 in square. Cut it into 10 × 10 cm/4 × 4 in wide strips, then cut the strips across to make 16 squares. Bring a large pan of salted water to the boil and cook the pieces of pasta, a few at a time if necessary, for 3 minutes. Drain and rinse under cold water, then lay out on double-thick absorbent kitchen paper.

Mix the ricotta, grated Parmesan, breadcrumbs, oregano and chopped watercress. Add seasoning and a little grated nutmeg to taste, then stir the mixture to make sure all the ingredients are thoroughly combined.

Set the oven at 200°C/400°F/Gas Mark 6. Butter an oven-proof dish. Place some of the cheese mixture on a piece of pasta, then roll it up into a neat tube and place in the dish with the end of the roll underneath. Repeat with the remaining pasta and filling. Ladle the tomato sauce over the cannelloni, then top with the mozzarella. Bake for 25–30 minutes, until the cheese has melted and browned. Use scissors to shred the basil leaves and soft stalks, and sprinkle over the cannelloni. Serve at once.

Aubergine Packages

Serves 4

Halve the quantities if you want to serve one package per person for a light main course or starter.

INGREDIENTS

2 small aubergines

salt and freshly ground black pepper

4–6 tbsp olive oil

2 large slices lean cooked ham

8 sage leaves

225 g/8 oz (8 small slices) dolcelatte cheese

⅔ quantity Pasta Dough (page 27)

2 large onions, thinly sliced

450 g/1 lb ripe tomatoes, peeled and sliced

100 g/4 oz soft cheese with garlic and herbs

100 g/4 oz fine dry white breadcrumbs

4 tbsp freshly grated Parmesan cheese

Trim the aubergines and cut eight slices. Layer these in a strainer with a little salt, place over a bowl, then leave to stand for 30 minutes. Rinse well and dry on absorbent kitchen paper.

Heat some olive oil in a frying pan and brown the aubergines on both sides, adding more oil as necessary. Cut the ham into eight pieces. Sandwich the aubergine slices in pairs, placing a piece of ham, sage leaf and slice of dolcelatte between each pair.

Roll out half the dough into a 30-cm/12-in square. Cut this into 10 × 15-cm/4 × 6-in squares, boil for 3 minutes and dry on double-thick absorbent kitchen paper. Place an aubergine sandwich in the centre of each square, then fold the pasta over it to make a neat package. Repeat with the remaining pasta and aubergines.

Set the oven at 180°C/350°F/Gas Mark 4. Heat any remaining olive oil. Add the onions and cook for 15–20 minutes, until softened. Spread the onions in the base of an oven-proof dish. Top with the tomatoes and season well. Arrange the aubergine packages on top, with the ends of the pasta dough underneath. Dot the tops of the packages with the soft cheese, spreading it slightly. Mix the breadcrumbs and Parmesan, then sprinkle some over the top of each package. Cover with greased aluminium foil. Bake for 20 minutes, then remove the foil and cook for a further 10 minutes.

CANNELLONI WITH CARROT AND COURGETTE

Serves 4

A vegetarian variation on a traditional pasta recipe.

INGREDIENTS

⅓ quantity Pasta Dough (page 27)

3 tbsp olive oil

1 onion, chopped

1 garlic clove, crushed

150 g/6 oz grated carrot

75 g/3 oz grated courgette

100 g/4 oz fresh white breadcrumbs

2 tomatoes, peeled and chopped

2 tbsp chopped fresh parsley

1 tsp dried marjoram

salt and freshly ground black pepper

1 quantity Cheese Sauce (page 43)

3 tbsp dry white breadcrumbs

Roll out the pasta thinly into a 41-cm/16-in square. Cut it into 10 × 10-cm/4 × 4-in wide strips, then cut the strips across four times to make 16 squares. Bring a large pan of salted water to the boil and cook the pieces of pasta, a few at a time if necessary, for 3 minutes. Drain and rinse under cold water, then lay out on double-thick absorbent kitchen paper.

Set the oven at 180°C/350°F/Gas Mark 4. Heat the oil in a large saucepan, add the onion and garlic and cook for 15 minutes, until the onion is softened but not browned. Stir in the carrots and continue to cook, stirring all the time, for a further 20 minutes, or until the carrots are tender. Regulate the heat to prevent the carrots from browning. Stir in the courgette, cook for 2–3 minutes, then remove the pan from the heat. Add the breadcrumbs, tomatoes, parsley, marjoram and seasoning to taste.

Place some of the vegetable mixture on a piece of pasta, then roll it up into a neat tube and place in the dish with the end of the roll underneath. Repeat with the remaining pasta and filling. Pour the cheese sauce over the cannelloni and sprinkle the breadcrumbs on top. Bake for 40 minutes in the pre-heated oven, until golden brown.

SEMOLINA CHEESE GNOCCHI

Serves 4

Gnocchi, small Italian dumplings, are usually grouped as close relatives of pasta. There are various ways of making gnocchi and using semolina is one common method.

INGREDIENTS

900 ml/1¾ pt milk

1 bay leaf

1 mace blade

150 g/6 oz semolina

100 g/4 oz freshly grated Parmesan cheese

salt and freshly ground black pepper

2 eggs

50 g/2 oz lightly salted butter

shredded basil or chopped fresh parsley, to serve

Pour the milk into a large pan and add the bay leaf and mace. Bring the milk slowly to the boil, then cover and remove from the heat. Allow the bay and mace to infuse for 45–60 minutes. Bring the milk back to just below boiling point, remove the bay and mace, then stir in the semolina. Cook, stirring all the time, until the mixture boils and thickens. It will become very stiff, so you have to work quite hard at stirring. This takes about 12–15 minutes.

Off the heat, beat in the Parmesan cheese and seasoning. Allow the mixture to cool slightly before beating in the eggs. Grease a baking sheet (a roasting tin will do) and spread the gnocchi mixture out so that it is about 1 cm/½ in thick. Cover, leave until completely cold, then chill for at least a couple of hours.

Set the oven at 200°C/400°F/Gas Mark 6. Use a little of the butter to grease an oven-proof dish. Cut the gnocchi into squares and arrange them in the dish. Melt the remaining butter and trickle it over the gnocchi. Bake for 20 minutes, until golden brown and crisp on top. Sprinkle with basil or parsley and serve at once.

Gnocchetti Sardi with Broccoli and Tomatoes

Serves 4

A lovely light lunch or supper dish. Choose vivid green, tightly packed heads of broccoli
and cook as briefly as possible to retain the colour and crisp texture.

INGREDIENTS

300 g/12 oz dried gnocchetti sardi
(small dumpling shapes)

dash of olive oil

65 g/2½ oz unsalted butter

300 g/¾ lb small broccoli florets

1 garlic clove, chopped

2 tsp chopped fresh rosemary

2 tsp chopped fresh oregano

salt and freshly ground black pepper

200 g/7 oz tin chopped tomatoes

1 tbsp tomato purée

fresh herbs, to garnish

Bring a large saucepan of water to the boil and add the gnocchetti sardi with a dash of olive oil. Cook for about 6 minutes, stirring occasionally, until tender. Drain and return to the saucepan, covered, to keep warm.

Meanwhile, melt the butter in a large frying pan and add the broccoli, garlic, rosemary, and oregano, and season with salt and freshly ground black pepper. Cover and cook gently for about 5 minutes, until tender.

Add the chopped tomatoes and tomato purée, and stir. Add the gnocchetti sardi, mix together lightly, then serve immediately, garnished with fresh herbs.

Potato Gnocchi

Serves 4

These may be served with Good Tomato Sauce (page 40), Pesto (page 40) or Cheese Sauce (page 43). If you are looking for a simple, satisfying supper, then simply toss them with butter, freshly ground black pepper, and lots of grated cheese – Parmesan or another type of your choice.

INGREDIENTS

450 g/1 lb potatoes

2 tbsp butter

150 g/6 oz strong flour

1 tsp salt

1 egg

a little freshly grated nutmeg

Parmesan cheese

Boil the potatoes in their skins until tender, about 20–30 minutes, depending on size. Drain and peel the potatoes under cold running water. Then mash them and sieve the mashed potato into a bowl.

Add the butter to the potato and mix well. Mix in the flour and salt, then add the egg and a little nutmeg. Mix the ingredients with a spoon at first, then use your hand to bring them together into a dough. Knead lightly until smooth.

Bring a large pan of salted water to the boil. Shape a lump of the dough into a thick sausage, then cut off small pieces, about 2.5 cm/1 in long, and indent each piece, either with your finger or with a fork. Drop the gnocchi into the boiling water, bring back to the boil and cook for 4–5 minutes. The water must not boil too rapidly and the cooked gnocchi should be firm and tender – do not overcook them or they will become soggy and watery. Use a slotted spoon to remove the gnocchi from the pan if you are cooking them in batches. Drain well and serve at once with melted butter, pepper, and freshly grated Parmesan.

WALNUT CHEESE RAVIOLI

Serves 6

For a special occasion, you could make the ravioli and sauce in advance and start cooking when your guests arrive.

INGREDIENTS

2 tbsp olive oil
1 small onion, finely chopped
1 garlic clove, crushed
100 g/4 oz finely chopped walnuts
100 g/4 oz ricotta cheese
75 g/3 oz gruyère cheese
2 tbsp freshly grated Parmesan cheese
6 basil sprigs, finely shredded
100 g/4 oz fresh white breadcrumbs
salt and freshly ground black pepper
⅔ quantity Pasta Dough (page 27)
1 egg, beaten
White Wine Sauce (page 42) or hot melted butter, to serve

Heat the olive oil in a small saucepan. Add the chopped onion and garlic and cook for 15 minutes, until the onion is softened but not browned. Remove from the heat, then stir in the chopped walnuts, ricotta, gruyère, grated Parmesan cheese, basil and breadcrumbs. Add seasoning to taste and mix the ingredients thoroughly.

Make the ravioli using the dough and beaten egg as for the Beef Ravioli with Tomato Sauce (page 106), making sure the mixture is well sealed in the dough. Cook the ravioli for 5 minutes in water which is just boiling, as the cheese filling does not take as long to cook as the raw beef filling. Drain and serve with White Wine Sauce or simply with butter and pepper.

SPINACH AND RICOTTA TORTELLINI

Serves 6–8

A vegetarian dish that is full of flavour. (Meat-eaters will love it too!)

INGREDIENTS

150 g/6 oz fresh spinach, trimmed and cooked

100 g/4 oz ricotta cheese

4 tbsp freshly grated Parmesan cheese

50 g/2 oz fresh white breadcrumbs

pinch of dried thyme

1 tsp dried marjoram

a little freshly grated nutmeg

salt and freshly ground black pepper

⅔ quantity Pasta Dough (page 27)

1 egg, beaten

Make sure the spinach is thoroughly drained, then chop it finely. Mix it with the ricotta, grated Parmesan, breadcrumbs and herbs. Add a little nutmeg and seasoning to taste.

Use the dough and beaten egg to make and fill the tortellini, following the instructions for Chicken Tortellini (page 116). Cook and serve the tortellini in the same way.

TORTELLINI, PEPPERS AND PINE NUT SALAD

Serves 4–6

Red peppers can be used instead of chillies, if you prefer. For best results,
allow the salad to chill for at least an hour before serving.

INGREDIENTS

300 g/12 oz fresh tortellini

dash of olive oil

1 onion, very finely sliced

1 green pepper, seeded and very finely
diced

65 g/2½ oz toasted pine nuts

1 red chilli, seeded and sliced
(optional)

10-cm/4-in piece of cucumber, very
thinly sliced

1 orange, peeled and very thinly sliced

DRESSING

4 tbsp olive oil

2 tbsp sweet soy sauce

2 tbsp vinegar

salt and freshly ground black pepper

Bring a large saucepan of water
to the boil and add the fresh
tortellini with a dash of olive oil. Cook
for about 4 minutes, stirring
occasionally, until tender. Drain and
rinse thoroughly under cold running
water. Drain again and set aside.

Place the tortellini in a large mixing
bowl and add the remaining salad
ingredients. Toss together lightly.

To make the salad dressing, place
all the dressing ingredients in a small
screw-top jar and shake well to
combine. Pour the dressing over the
salad, toss and serve.

Pasta with Beans and Lentils

PASTA BEAN SOUP

Serves 4–6

A nutritious meal in itself – low-fat and full of protein. Serve with warm, crusty garlic bread.

INGREDIENTS

2 tbsp olive oil

3 garlic cloves, crushed

4 tbsp chopped fresh parsley

300 g/12 oz dried whole wheat gnocchi piccoli (shells)

1⅓ litre/2¾ pints vegetable stock

3 tbsp vegetable purée or tomato purée

400 g/14 oz tin mixed beans, such as borlotti, kidney, cannellini etc, drained

salt and freshly ground black pepper

freshly grated Parmesan cheese, to serve

Heat the olive oil in a large saucepan and sauté the garlic with the chopped parsley for about 2 minutes. Add the gnocchi piccoli and cook for 1–2 minutes, stirring constantly.

Pour in the stock and add the vegetable or tomato purée. Bring to the boil, reduce the heat, then simmer for about 10 minutes, stirring occasionally, until the pasta is tender.

Add the beans and season with salt and freshly ground black pepper. Continue to cook for a further 5 minutes, then serve with a little freshly grated Parmesan cheese.

FUSILLI WITH KIDNEY BEANS

Serves 4–6

The chilli flavouring in this dish can be adjusted according to taste.

INGREDIENTS

450 g/1 lb dried fusilli

dash of olive oil

2 × 400 g/14 oz tins chopped tomatoes

1 onion, sliced

3 tbsp chopped fresh parsley

pinch of chilli powder

salt and freshly ground black pepper

2 tbsp tomato purée

dry red wine

400 g/14 oz tin red kidney beans

Bring a large saucepan of water to the boil and add the fusilli with a dash of olive oil. Cook for about 10 minutes, stirring occasionally, until tender. Drain and set aside.

Place all the remaining ingredients, except the kidney beans, in a large

frying pan and bring to the boiling point. Reduce the heat and simmer for 10 minutes, until the liquid has reduced and the onion has softened.

Add the fusilli and kidney beans to the tomato mixture. Stir, cover and cook for about 5minutes, stirring occasionally. Serve immediately.

Pasta Bean Soup ▶

LENTIL PASTA BURGERS

Serves 2–4

Served with pitta bread and a little salad, these make a treat for children.

INGREDIENTS

65 g/2½ oz dried pastina (any tiny shapes)

dash of olive oil

200 g/7 oz tin brown lentils, drained

4 tbsp dried whole wheat breadcrumbs

40 g/1½ oz finely grated fresh Parmesan cheese

1 small onion, chopped

1 tbsp chopped fresh parsley

4 tbsp crunchy peanut butter

1 tbsp tomato purée

1 tsp yeast extract

4 tbsp hot water

sunflower oil, for shallow frying

Bring a large saucepan of water to the boil, and add the pastina with a dash of olive oil. Cook for about 8 minutes, stirring occasionally, until the pasta is tender. Drain and allow to cool slightly.

Combine the pasta in a large mixing bowl with the lentils, breadcrumbs, grated Parmesan cheese, chopped onion and fresh parsley.

Place the peanut butter, tomato purée and yeast extract in a separate bowl, and stir together with the hot water. Add this to the lentil mixture, and mix well.

Using damp hands, divide the mixture into four equal portions, and form into burger shapes. Heat the sunflower oil for shallow frying and fry the burgers for about 5 minutes on each side. Serve hot or cold with pitta bread and salad.

SMOKED TOFU WITH SQUARES

Serves 4

Pasta flavoured with herbs or tomatoes goes very well with smoked tofu. If you do not want to make your own pasta, buy fresh fusilli or *paglia e fieno* (straw and hay).

INGREDIENTS

2 tbsp olive oil

2 tbsp butter

4 celery stalks, finely diced

1 green pepper, seeded and diced

salt and freshly ground black pepper

450 g/1 lb smoked tofu (bean curd), cut into small cubes

zest of 1 lemon

2 spring onions, finely chopped

3 tbsp chopped fresh parsley

450 g/1 lb fresh small pasta squares

lemon wedges, to serve

Heat the oil and butter in a large saucepan. Add the celery and cook, stirring, for 5 minutes. Add the green pepper, a little salt and plenty of freshly ground black pepper, stir well and cook gently for a further 10 minutes. Lightly mix the tofu into the pepper and celery mixture, then leave to heat through for about 5 minutes.

Mix the lemon zest, spring onions and parsley. Toss the freshly cooked, drained pasta with the tofu mixture, and serve in individual bowls. Sprinkle with the lemon zest, spring onions and parsley mixture. Serve with lemon wedges. The juice from the lemon may be squeezed over the pasta.

Lentil and Mushroom Cannelloni

Serves 4

The tomato cannelloni is not essential, but adds to the attractive colour of the finished dish.
Dried cannelloni tubes work just as well.

INGREDIENTS

⅓ quantity Pasta Dough (page 27), with 1 tbsp tomato purée beaten into the eggs

dash of olive oil, plus 3 tbsp

250 g/10 oz brown lentils, washed and drained

3 garlic cloves, crushed

2 tbsp dried thyme

2 × quantity Mushroom Sauce (see below)

125 g/5 oz grated Cheddar cheese

chopped fresh parsley, to garnish

Roll out the pasta dough thinly to a 41-cm/16-inch square, and cut it into four 10-cm/4-inch wide strips. Cut the strips across to make 16 squares.

Bring a large saucepan of water to the boil, and add the squares of pasta in batches with a dash of olive oil. Cook for about 3 minutes. Drain, and rinse under cold running water. Pat dry with absorbent kitchen paper and set aside.

Bring another large saucepan of water to the boil and add the lentils. Cook for about 30 minutes, stirring occasionally, until tender. Drain and rinse under boiling water. Drain again and set aside. Pre-heat oven to 180°C/350°F/Gas Mark 4.

Heat the remaining olive oil in a large frying pan and sauté the garlic and thyme for about 2 minutes. Add the lentils, stir and cook for about 5 minutes. Remove from the heat, and set aside to cool slightly.

Place a little of the lentil mixture along one edge of each piece of pasta, and roll up to form a neat tube. Arrange the cannelloni in a shallow, oven-proof dish, sides down. Pour the mushroom sauce over the cannelloni and sprinkle with grated cheese. Bake for about 40 minutes, until bubbling and golden. Serve garnished with chopped fresh parsley.

Mushroom Sauce

Makes 600 ml/1 pint

INGREDIENTS

2 tbsp butter or margarine

25 g/1 oz plain flour

600 ml/1 pint warm milk

115 g/4½ oz chopped button mushrooms

2 tbsp olive oil

1 garlic clove, crushed

pinch of dried thyme

salt and freshly ground black pepper

Melt the butter or margarine in a medium-sized saucepan, and stir in the flour. Cook for 30 seconds, then remove from the heat. Stir in the milk, a little at a time, blending well after each addition. Return to a medium heat, and stir until the sauce thickens and boils.

Sauté the mushrooms in the olive oil, together with the garlic and thyme, and add to the sauce. Season to taste. Continue to cook, stirring constantly until thoroughly blended.

Lentil and Mushroom Cannelloni ▶

BEAN CURRY WITH LASAGNETTE

Serves 4–6

Lasagnette is a longer, thinner version of lasagne. Any form of noodles works well to serve with this recipe.

INGREDIENTS

300 g/12 oz lasagnette

dash of olive oil, plus 2 tbsp oil

2 garlic cloves, crushed

1 onion, chopped

3–4 tbsp mild curry paste

3 tbsp chopped fresh coriander

300 ml/½ pint vegetable stock

2 × 400 g/14 oz tins mixed beans, such as black-eyed, flageolet, cannellini, etc, drained

chopped fresh coriander

lime slices, to garnish

Bring a large saucepan of water to the boil and add the lasagnette with a dash of olive oil. Cook for about 10 minutes, stirring occasionally, until tender. Drain and return to the saucepan. Cover to keep warm.

Heat the remaining olive oil in a large saucepan and sauté the garlic and onion for about 5 minutes, stirring occasionally. Stir in the curry paste, and cook for a further 2–3 minutes. Add the chopped coriander and vegetable stock, and cook for 5 minutes. Stir in the beans, cover and cook for 10 minutes, stirring occasionally.

Serve the curry with the lasagnette, sprinkled with chopped fresh coriander and garnished with lime slices.

SAUTÉED FLAGEOLET BEANS WITH FUSILLI

Serves 2–4

A garlicky dish, made with fresh tarragon to enhance the delicate flavors. Serve as a main course or as an accompaniment.

INGREDIENTS

700 g/1½ lb dried fusilli

dash of olive oil, plus 4 tbsp oil

3 garlic cloves, crushed

1 large onion, sliced

2 tbsp chopped fresh tarragon

400 g/14 oz tin flageolet beans, drained

salt and freshly ground black pepper

Bring a large saucepan of water to the boil and add the fusilli with a dash of olive oil. Cook for about 10 minutes, stirring occasionally, until tender. Drain and set aside.

Heat the remaining olive oil in a large frying pan and sauté the garlic and onion for about 5 minutes, until the onion has browned slightly. Add the tarragon and beans, and season with salt and freshly ground black pepper. Cook for 2–3 minutes, then stir in the fusilli. Cook for 3–5 minutes, to heat through. Serve with a crisp green salad.

WINTER STEW

Serves 4

You can give this vegetarian dish to carnivores – they'll never notice the lack of meat.

INGREDIENTS

250 g/9 oz dried whole-wheat radiatori

dash of olive oil, plus 2 tbsp oil

2 garlic cloves, crushed

1 onion, chopped

5–6 carrots, cut into 1-cm/½-inch chunks

150 g/6 oz button mushrooms

400 g/14 oz tin chopped tomatoes

2 × 400 g/14 oz tins red and black kidney beans, drained

300 ml/½ pint vegetable stock

1 tbsp paprika

2 tbsp sweet soy sauce

salt and freshly ground black pepper

1 tbsp cornflour

Bring a large saucepan of water to the boil and add the radiatori with a dash of olive oil. Cook for about 10 minutes, stirring occasionally, until tender. Drain and set aside.

Heat the remaining olive oil in a large saucepan and sauté the garlic and onion for about 3 minutes, stirring occasionally. Add the carrots and cook for about 5 minutes.

Add the mushrooms and continue to cook for about 3 minutes, stirring occasionally, until slightly softened. Add the remaining ingredients, except the cornflour, and stir in the radiatori. Cover and cook gently for about 15 minutes, until vegetables are tender.

In a small bowl, mix the cornflour with a little of the cooking liquid to make a smooth paste. Add the cornflour paste to the stew. Stir and allow to boil again, stirring constantly, until thickened. Cook for a final 3 minutes before serving.

Sautéed Flageolet Beans with Fusilli ▶

CONTINENTAL LENTIL SOUP

Serves 4–6

Tinned lentils make this soup even easier to prepare. They are available from most good delicatessens.

INGREDIENTS

50 g/2 oz butter

2 garlic cloves, crushed

65 g/2½ oz dried pastina (any tiny shapes)

4 tbsp finely chopped fresh parsley

400 g/14 oz tin brown lentils, drained

1⅓ litre/2¾ pints vegetable stock

salt and freshly ground black pepper

freshly grated Parmesan cheese, to serve (optional)

Melt the butter in a large saucepan and sauté the crushed garlic cloves for about 2 minutes, stirring occasionally.

Add the pastina and chopped parsley and stir. Cook for a further 2–3 minutes, then add the lentils and stock and season with salt and freshly ground black pepper.

Bring the soup to the boil, then reduce the heat and simmer for about 15 minutes. Serve with a little freshly grated Parmesan cheese, if wished.

STUFFED PASTA SHELLS

Serves 4–6

These are great as an appetizer or served as a canapé with drinks at a party. They can be made in advance
and served cold, or re-heated in the oven to serve warm.

INGREDIENTS

12 dried conchiglie rigate

dash of olive oil

FILLING

225 g/8 oz brown lentils, washed and
drained

2 garlic cloves, crushed

400 g/14 oz tin chopped tomatoes

1 tbsp tomato purée

3 tbsp chopped fresh basil

60 ml/2½ fl oz dry red wine

salt and freshly ground black pepper

TOPPING

4 tbsp fine dried bread crumbs

50 g/2 oz finely grated fresh Parmesan
cheese

3 tbsp chopped fresh parsley

Bring a large saucepan of water to the boil and add the conchiglie rigate with a dash of olive oil. Cook for about 10 minutes, stirring occasionally, until tender. Drain and rinse under cold running water. Drain again and lay out on absorbent kitchen paper.

To make the filling, bring a large saucepan of water to the boil and add the lentils. Simmer for about 30 minutes, until tender. Drain and rinse under boiling water.

Place the garlic, chopped tomatoes, tomato purée, chopped fresh basil, wine, and salt and freshly ground black pepper in a large frying pan. Bring to the boiling point, then reduce the heat and simmer for 2–3 minutes. Add the lentils, stir and cook for about a further

10 minutes, until all the moisture has evaporated and the mixture has thickened.

Use a teaspoon to stuff the pasta shells with the filling mixture, and arrange them on a baking sheet. Combine the topping ingredients together in a small bowl, and sprinkle over the stuffed shells. Place in a hot grill for about 5 minutes, until golden.

Vegetable Dishes

PASTA-TOPPED MUSHROOMS

Serves 2–4

This dish is delicious served cold with a crisp leafy salad, or warm as an appetizer or an accompaniment.
The topping can be made in advance and arranged on the mushrooms at the last minute.

INGREDIENTS

50 g/2 oz dried stelline

dash of olive oil

4 large flat mushrooms

50 g/2 oz butter

I garlic clove, crushed

½ yellow pepper,
seeded and finely diced

½ orange pepper,
seeded and finely diced

100 g/4 oz blue cheese, such as Stilton
or Danish blue, crumbled

salt and freshly ground black pepper

2 tbsp chopped fresh parsley

Bring a large saucepan of water to the boil and add the pasta with a dash of olive oil. Cook for about 7 minutes, stirring occasionally, until tender. Drain and set aside.

Cut the stems out of the mushrooms and discard. Arrange the mushrooms, stem side up, on a baking sheet and set aside.

To make the topping, melt the butter in a frying pan and sauté the garlic for about 2 minutes. Add the diced peppers and cook for a further 5–7 minutes. Stir in the crumbled blue cheese and season to taste with salt and freshly ground black pepper. Add the parsley and pasta. Stir well.

Top each mushroom with the pasta mixture, then place the baking sheet in the grill for 2–5 minutes, or until the topping is lightly golden and the mushrooms are warmed through.

STUFFED PEPPERS

Serves 4

A refreshing alternative to rice, pasta makes a perfect filling for peppers. Tiny pasta shapes also work well in this dish.
Serve with a crisp, green salad.

INGREDIENTS

225 g/8 oz gnocchetti sardi (small dumpling shapes)

dash of olive oil

4 peppers, for stuffing

flat leaf parsley sprigs, to garnish

FILLING

50 g/2 oz butter

6 spring onions, finely chopped

2 garlic cloves, crushed

1 pepper, seeded and finely diced

salt and freshly ground black pepper

65 g/2½ oz freshly grated Parmesan cheese

Bring a large saucepan of water to the boil and add the gnocchetti sardi with a dash of olive oil. Cook for about 10 minutes, stirring occasionally, until tender. Drain and set aside.

Preheat the oven to 200°C/400°F/Gas Mark 6. Lay each pepper on its side and slice off the top, reserving it to make the lid. Scoop out and discard the seeds and pith. Arrange the hollowed-out peppers in a shallow, oven-proof dish, and set aside.

To make the filling, melt the butter in a large frying pan and sauté the spring onions and garlic for about 2 minutes, then add the diced pepper. Season with salt and freshly ground black pepper and cook for about 5 minutes, stirring occasionally.

Add the gnocchetti and the Parmesan cheese to the filling mixture, and cook for about 2 minutes to heat through. Using a dessertspoon, stuff each pepper with the pasta filling, scattering any extra around the edges.

Place the pepper lids in the dish. Bake for about 30 minutes, until the peppers have softened. Just before serving, place under the grill for 2–3 minutes to char the pepper skins, if desired. Garnish with parsley sprigs.

PEPPER AND PASTA RATATOUILLE

Serves 4–6

Served with a hot, buttered baked potato, this simple dish is perfectly delicious.

INGREDIENTS

450 g/1 lb dried whole-wheat gnocchi piccoli (small shells)

dash of olive oil, plus 3 tbsp oil

2 garlic cloves, crushed

1 onion, chopped

2 green peppers, seeded and cut into chunks

400 g/14 oz tin chopped tomatoes

2 heaped tbsp tomato purée

180 ml/6½ fl oz dry red wine

2 tbsp fresh oregano

salt and freshly ground black pepper

fresh oregano sprigs, to garnish

Bring a large saucepan of water to the boil and add the whole-wheat gnocchi piccoli with a dash of olive oil. Cook for about 10 minutes, stirring occasionally, until tender. Drain and set aside.

Heat the remaining olive oil in a large saucepan and sauté the garlic and chopped onion for about 3 minutes, until softened. Stir in the pepper chunks. Cover and cook for about 5 minutes, or until the pepper has softened slightly.

Stir in the remaining ingredients, except the oregano sprigs, into the pepper mixture and bring to simmering point. Reduce the heat, cover and cook for about 10 minutes, then stir in the gnocchi piccoli. Cook for a further 5 minutes, stirring occasionally. Serve garnished with fresh oregano sprigs.

COCONUT VEGETABLES WITH PASTA

Serves 4–6

Make this dish a day ahead to allow the flavours to develop.
Creamed coconut is available from most supermarkets and ethnic grocers.

INGREDIENTS

3 tbsp olive oil

2 garlic cloves, crushed

1 onion, chopped

2 tsp ground cumin

2 tsp ground coriander

225 g/½ lb creamed coconut, chopped

625 ml/25 fl oz boiling water

salt and freshly ground black pepper

1 vegetable stock cube

3 carrots, diced

2 small courgettes, diced

5 celery stalks, chopped

½ small cauliflower, separated into florets

16 baby corn cobs

5 tbsp chopped fresh coriander

300 g/12 oz fresh linguini

Heat the olive oil in a large skillet and sauté the garlic, onion, cumin and coriander for about 3 minutes, stirring occasionally, until the onion has softened.

Add the creamed coconut to the boiling water. Stir well, and season with salt and freshly ground black pepper. Add the stock cube, and stir until dissolved. Add the vegetables and coriander to the pan, and stir well. Cover and simmer for 15–20 minutes, stirring occasionally, until the vegetables are tender. Remove the cover and continue to cook for about 5 minutes, until the sauce has thickened slightly.

Meanwhile, bring a large saucepan of water to the boil, and add the fresh linguini with a dash of olive oil. Cook for about 4 minutes, stirring occasionally, until tender. Drain and serve with the vegetables.

FRESH GREEN PASTA

Serves 4

This combination of ingredients also makes an excellent salad. If you use very small pasta squares, the hot mixture may also be served in scooped-out tomatoes as a first course.

INGREDIENTS

300 g/12 oz shelled or frozen peas

4 tbsp olive oil or 50 g/2 oz butter

4 spring onions, chopped

2 avocados, halved and cut into chunks

juice of ½ lemon

salt and freshly ground black pepper

450 g/1 lb fresh pasta verdi

1 tbsp chopped fresh mint

Cook the peas in boiling salted water for 10 minutes. Heat the oil or melt the butter in a saucepan.

Add the spring onions and cook for 1 minute, then stir in the peas, avocado and lemon juice. Season to taste.

Toss the pea and avocado mixture into the freshly cooked drained pasta. Sprinkle with mint and serve at once. Mint sprigs may be added as a garnish if liked.

ASPARAGUS SUPREME

Serves 4

This is really simple and quite unbeatable, especially if you are able to raid a pick-your-own farm for the freshest possible asparagus, and cook the vegetable whilst it still spits with zest when you snap the stems. If you are health-conscious, toss the asparagus in 1 tablespoon of hot olive oil and mix some yoghurt into the pasta instead of using lots and lots of butter!

INGREDIENTS

450 g/1 lb asparagus, trimmed of woody ends if necessary

6 tbsp butter

salt and freshly ground black pepper

450 g/1 lb fresh tagliatelle verde or spinach-flavoured small pasta squares

3 tbsp chopped fresh dill

freshly grated Parmesan cheese, to serve (optional)

Cook the asparagus in boiling salted water for 10–20 minutes, until just tender. If you do not have a tall asparagus saucepan, use the deepest pan you have. Put the asparagus in it so that the tips stand above the rim. Place foil in a tent shape over the top of the pan, crumpling it securely around the rim to seal in the steam. Very fresh, young asparagus will cook in 10 minutes; larger or more mature stems take longer.

Heat the butter whilst the pasta is cooking. Drain the asparagus and cut the stems into short lengths, then add them to the butter. Add a little seasoning, then pour the asparagus mixture over the drained pasta. Sprinkle with dill and mix well. Serve at once with freshly grated Parmesan, if you like.

ITALIAN SPAGHETTINI

Serves 4

Pine nuts give this dish its special taste and texture. Serve it straight from the pan.

INGREDIENTS

450 g/1 lb dried multicoloured spaghettini

dash of olive oil

50 g/2 oz butter

1 garlic clove, crushed

1 small onion, very finely chopped

65 g/2½ oz pine nuts

100 g/4 oz sieved tomatoes

4 tbsp chopped fresh basil

2 tbsp chopped fresh parsley

salt and freshly ground black pepper

Bring a large saucepan of water to the boil. Add the pasta with a dash of olive oil. Cook for about 10 minutes, stirring occasionally, until tender. Drain and set aside.

Melt the butter in a large frying pan and sauté the garlic and onion for about 3 minutes, or until the onion has softened. Add the pine nuts and stir-fry until evenly golden.

Add the sieved tomatoes, herbs and salt and freshly ground black pepper and cook for about 5 minutes, stirring occasionally.

Add the spaghettini and stir well to coat in the tomato sauce. Cook for a further 5 minutes, then serve immediately.

EGG AND TOMATO FAVOURITE

Serves 4

Familiar foods that go together well make this slightly unusual, yet reassuringly homely dish.

INGREDIENTS

450 g/1 lb tomatoes, peeled and roughly chopped

salt and freshly ground black pepper

4 tbsp chopped fresh parsley

8 eggs

large knob of butter

450 g/1 lb fresh pasta

freshly grated Parmesan or Cheddar cheese, to serve

Place the tomatoes in a bowl and season them well, then mix in the parsley. Place the eggs in a saucepan, cover with cold water and bring to the boil. Cook for 10 minutes, then drain. Shell the eggs under cold water so as not to burn your fingers and place them in a bowl, then cut them into eighths.

Toss the hot eggs and butter into the freshly cooked, drained pasta, then mix in the tomatoes when the butter has melted. Serve at once, topping each portion with grated cheese.

TAGLIATELLE WITH SESAME CABBAGE

Serves 4

Herb-flavoured tagliatelle is ideal for this recipe.

INGREDIENTS

4 tbsp sunflower oil

1 large onion, chopped

1 garlic clove, crushed

3 tbsp sesame seeds

3 tbsp currants

salt and freshly ground black pepper

450 g/1 lb red or white cabbage, shredded

1 tbsp cider vinegar

450 g/1 lb fresh tagliatelle

Heat the oil, then add the onion, garlic, sesame seeds and currants. Add seasoning to taste. Cook, stirring often, over moderate to low heat for about 20 minutes, until the onion is well cooked. Stir in the cabbage and cook for about 10 minutes, stirring often so that the cabbage is lightly cooked and still crunchy. Add the vinegar and stir well.

Toss the cabbage mixture with the freshly cooked, drained tagliatelle and serve at once.

BUCKWHEAT NOODLES WITH SAVOY CABBAGE

Serves 6

Buckwheat noodles, known as 'pizzoccheri', are a speciality of northern Italy, and are available from some Italian delicatessens. Whole-wheat or egg tagliatelle make good substitutes.

INGREDIENTS

300 g/12 oz dried buckwheat noodles

225 g/½ lb savoy cabbage, shredded

1 medium potato, peeled and diced

dash of olive oil

100 g/4 oz plus 2 tbsp unsalted butter

2 garlic cloves, chopped

4 tbsp chopped fresh sage

pinch of freshly grated nutmeg

scant 225 g/½ lb Fontina cheese, diced

100 g/4 oz freshly grated Parmesan cheese

Bring a large saucepan of water to the boil and add the buckwheat noodles, cabbage and potato with a dash of olive oil. Cook for 10–15 minutes, stirring occasionally, until tender. Drain and set aside, covered, to keep warm.

Meanwhile, melt the butter in a large frying pan and sauté the garlic and sage for about 1 minute. Remove from the heat and set aside.

Place a layer of the pasta and vegetables in a warm serving dish, and sprinkle with a little nutmeg, some of the Fontina and some of the Parmesan cheese.

Repeat the layers, then pour the hot garlic butter over the pasta. Mix lightly into the pasta and serve immediately.

Tagliatelle with Sesame Cabbage ▶

BUCATINI WITH TOMATOES

Serves 4

This is a vegetarian version of a simple yet classic Italian dish. Use Parmesan cheese if Romano is not available.

INGREDIENTS

300 g/12 oz dried bucatini

dash of olive oil

2 garlic cloves, crushed

1 onion, finely chopped

225 g/8 oz sieved tomatoes

4 tbsp chopped fresh basil

salt and freshly ground black pepper

butter, for greasing

65 g/2½ oz freshly grated Romano or Parmesan cheese

Bring a large saucepan of water to the boil and add the bucatini with a dash of olive oil. Cook for about 10 minutes, stirring occasionally, until tender. Drain and set aside.

Pre-heat the oven to 200°C/400°F/Gas Mark 6. Place the garlic, onion, sieved tomatoes, basil and salt and freshly ground black pepper in a large frying pan and heat until simmering. Cook for about 5 minutes, then remove from the heat.

Arrange the bucatini in a shallow, buttered, oven-proof dish. Curl it around to fit the dish, adding one or two tubes at a time, until the dish is tightly packed with the pasta.

Spoon the tomato mixture over the top, prodding the pasta to ensure the sauce sinks down to the bottom of the dish. Sprinkle with the grated cheese. Bake for 25–30 minutes, until bubbling, crisp and golden. Cut in wedges like a cake to serve.

TAGLIATELLE WITH MUSHROOMS

Serves 4

A quick supper for any occasion. Try using spaghetti or linguini for a change.

INGREDIENTS

450 g/1 lb dried tagliatelle

dash of olive oil

2 tbsp butter

1 garlic clove, crushed

2 tbsp chopped fresh parsley

150 g/6 oz button or cup mushrooms, sliced

salt and freshly ground black pepper

300 ml/½ pint single cream

freshly grated Parmesan cheese, to serve

Bring a large saucepan of water to the boil and add the tagliatelle with a dash of olive oil. Cook for about 10 minutes, stirring occasionally, until tender. Drain and set aside.

Meanwhile, melt the butter in a large frying pan and sauté the garlic and chopped parsley for 2–3 minutes.

Add the sliced mushrooms and cook for 5–8 minutes, or until softened and slightly browned.

Season the mushroom mixture with salt and freshly ground black pepper, then stir in the cream. Cook the sauce for 1–2 minutes, then stir in the freshly cooked tagliatelle. Continue to cook whilst stirring to coat the tagliatelle in the mushroom sauce. Serve with plenty of freshly grated Parmesan cheese.

SPAGHETTI MORGAN

Serves 6

The pungent flavour of the aubergine and the virtually uncooked strands of basil make this sauce truly special.
It originates from Sicily.

INGREDIENTS

300 ml/½ pint olive oil

3 garlic cloves, crushed

1 medium onion, sliced

900 g/2 lb fresh plum or canned
tomatoes

1 tsp sugar

1 large aubergine

2 tbsp finely chopped fresh basil

450 g/1 lb spaghetti

Heat 4 tablespoons of olive oil in a deep frying pan and cook the crushed garlic and onion to soften. Roughly chop the tomatoes and add to the pan. Add the sugar and turn the heat down to simmer.

In a deepish pan, heat the remaining olive oil until just below smoking temperature. As the oil heats up, cut the aubergine into small 5 mm/ ¼ inch dice. Fry the aubergine dice, a batch at a time, until the flesh is cooked to a wrinkled mid-brown. Set aside the cooked pieces on absorbent kitchen paper. Stir the aubergine into the tomato sauce and add the finely chopped basil. Check the seasoning and serve with the freshly cooked, drained spaghetti.

MINESTRONE SOUP

Serves 4–6

There are many different versions of this classic soup; this one is simple, wholesome and filling.
Serve with warm, crusty garlic bread.

INGREDIENTS

5 tbsp extra virgin olive oil

3 garlic cloves, crushed

6 carrots, finely diced

3 medium courgettes, finely diced

65 g/2½ oz dried pastina

5 tbsp chopped fresh parsley

2 tbsp vegetable purée

1⅓ litre/2¾ pints good vegetable stock

salt and freshly ground black pepper

freshly grated Parmesan cheese,
to serve

Heat the extra virgin olive oil in a large saucepan and add the crushed garlic. Sauté for about 2 minutes, then stir in the diced carrots and courgettes. Cook for about 5 minutes, stirring occasionally.

Stir the pastina and chopped parsley into the vegetable mixture, add the vegetable purée and vegetable stock, and season with salt and freshly ground black pepper.

Cover and simmer for about 30 minutes, until the vegetables and pasta have softened and the flavours have developed. Pour the soup into bowls and sprinkle with the freshly grated Parmesan cheese.

PASTA WITH EGGS AND TARRAGON

Serves 4

An easy dish that makes a tasty change from poached eggs on toast! Serve half portions for a starter or light snack.

INGREDIENTS

6 tbsp butter (or use olive oil or a mixture of butter and olive oil if preferred)

3 tbsp chopped fresh tarragon

8 eggs

450 g/1 lb fresh pasta (tagliatelle or fusilli)

freshly ground black pepper

freshly grated Parmesan cheese,

Warm four plates or bowls. Melt the butter (or heat the oil with the butter if used) and add the chopped fresh tarragon, then set aside over very low heat. Poach the eggs when the pasta is just cooked and ready for draining.

Divide the freshly cooked, drained pasta between the plates or bowls. Place a couple of eggs on each portion, then spoon the butter and tarragon over the top. Season with black pepper and serve at once with grated Parmesan cheese.

RIGATONI WITH PEPPERS AND GARLIC

Serves 4

The raw garlic added at the end of the recipe gives this dish the true taste of the Mediterranean.

INGREDIENTS

300 g/12 oz dried rigatoni

dash of olive oil, plus 4 tbsp

1 large onion, chopped

4 garlic cloves, finely chopped

2 large red peppers, seeded and roughly chopped

2 large yellow peppers, seeded and roughly chopped

2 tsp chopped fresh thyme

salt and freshly ground black pepper

Bring a large saucepan of water to the boil and add the rigatoni with a dash of olive oil. Cook for about 10 minutes, stirring occasionally, until tender. Drain and set aside.

Heat the remaining oil in a large frying pan and add the chopped onion, two cloves of garlic, peppers and thyme. Cook over a medium heat for 10–15 minutes, stirring occasionally, until the vegetables are tender and beginning to brown.

Add the pasta shapes to the pepper mixture. Stir in the remaining garlic and seasoning. Serve immediately.

Pasta with Eggs and Tarragon ▶

PASTA WITH MIXED MUSHROOMS

Serves 4

Dried mushrooms (*porcini*) are available in all good Italian delis.

INGREDIENTS

40 g/1½ oz dried mushrooms

300 ml/½ pint dry white wine

50 g/2 oz butter

225 g/8 oz crimini mushrooms, sliced

225 g/8 oz oyster mushrooms, sliced

300 ml/½ pint single cream

salt and freshly ground black pepper

3 tbsp chopped fresh parsley

450 g/1 lb fresh pasta

freshly grated Parmesan cheese, to serve

Place the dried mushrooms in a bowl and pour the wine over them. Cover with a saucer and weight it down to keep the mushrooms submerged in the wine. Leave for 30 minutes. Discard any tough stems and slice the mushrooms if necessary (they are usually sold sliced in packages).

Melt the butter in a large saucepan. Add the crimini mushrooms and cook for 5 minutes, stirring. Pour in the dried mushrooms and wine from soaking. Bring to the boil, reduce the heat and cook at a steady simmer for 15 minutes. Stir in the oyster mushrooms, cook for 2–3 minutes, then add the cream, seasoning and parsley. Heat gently, stirring, but do not boil or the sauce will curdle.

Add the freshly cooked, drained pasta to the sauce, remove from the heat and mix well. Allow to stand, covered, for 2–3 minutes, then toss the pasta again and serve with grated Parmesan cheese.

MALTAGLIATI WITH TOMATO TARRAGON CREAM

Serves 4

This rich pasta dish is not for the health conscious!
However, it is extremely delicious with a glass of chilled dry white wine.

INGREDIENTS

450 g/1 lb dried maltagliati
dash of olive oil, plus 1 tbsp
2 garlic cloves, crushed
4 tbsp chopped fresh tarragon
225 g/½ lb cherry tomatoes, halved
300 ml/½ pint single cream
salt and freshly ground black pepper
freshly grated Parmesan cheese, to serve

Bring a large saucepan of water to the boil and add the maltagliati with a dash of olive oil. Cook for about 10 minutes, stirring occasionally, until tender. Drain the pasta and return to the saucepan. Set aside, covered, to keep warm.

Heat the remaining olive oil in a large frying pan and add the garlic, tarragon and tomatoes. Sauté for about 3 minutes, stirring occasionally, then stir in the cream. Season with salt and freshly ground black pepper and cook for 2–3 minutes, until heated through. Stir into the pasta, then serve with freshly grated Parmesan cheese.

VEGETABLE AND CORIANDER SOUP

Serves 4–6

A light, fresh-tasting soup that is ideal either as an appetizer or as a light lunch.

INGREDIENTS

1¼ litres/2 pints vegetable stock

300 g/12 oz dried pasta

dash of olive oil

2 carrots, thinly sliced

250 g/10 oz frozen peas

6 tbsp chopped fresh coriander

salt and freshly ground black pepper

Bring the vegetable stock to the boil in a large saucepan and add the dried pasta with a dash of olive oil to the pan. Cook for about 5 minutes, stirring occasionally, then add the thinly sliced carrots.

Cook for 5 minutes, then add the peas and coriander. Season with salt and freshly ground black pepper and simmer gently for about 10 minutes, stirring occasionally, until the pasta and carrots are tender. Serve the soup with finely grated cheese, if wished.

Baby Cauliflower and Broccoli Cheese

Serves 4

Baby vegetables can be both formal and fun. To make this recipe suitable for children,
omit the wine and cream from the sauce.

INGREDIENTS

300 g/12 oz dried casareccia

dash of olive oil

50 g/2 oz butter

salt and freshly ground black pepper

6 mini cauliflowers

6 mini broccoli spears

1 quantity Cheese Sauce (below)

3 tbsp dry white wine

2 tbsp double cream

125 g/5 oz grated mature Cheddar
cheese

Bring a large saucepan of water to the boil and add the casareccia with a dash of olive oil. Cook for about 10 minutes, stirring occasionally, until tender. Drain and return to the saucepan with the butter, and season with salt and ground black pepper. Cover and set aside to keep warm.

Bring a large saucepan of water to the boil and add the baby cauliflowers and baby broccoli spears. Cook for about 5 minutes, until tender. Drain and return to the saucepan, covered, to keep warm.

Place the cheese sauce in a saucepan and stir in the wine and cream. Heat gently, stirring constantly, for about 5 minutes.

To serve, divide the pasta between four warmed individual plates and arrange the baby vegetables on top. Pour the cheese sauce over the pasta, and sprinkle with grated cheese. Serve immediately.

CHEESE SAUCE

Makes about 600 ml/1 pint

This sauce will keep in the refrigerator for up to a week.

INGREDIENTS

2 tbsp butter or margarine

25 g/1 oz plain flour

600 ml/1 pint warm milk

1 tsp Dijon mustard

150 g/6 oz grated mature Cheddar cheese

salt and freshly ground black pepper

Melt the butter or margarine in a medium-sized saucepan, and stir in the flour. Cook for 30 seconds, then remove from the heat.

Stir in the milk, a little at a time, blending well after each addition to prevent any lumps. Return the sauce to a medium heat, and stir constantly until the sauce thickens and boils.

Add the mustard and cheese, and season to taste with salt and freshly ground black pepper. Continue to cook, stirring constantly, until the cheese has melted.

VERDE VEGETABLES WITH VERMICELLI

Serves 4–6

A wonderful summer dish to be eaten warm or cold, with chunks of crusty French bread.

INGREDIENTS

300 g/12 oz dried vermicelli

dash of olive oil

2 tbsp butter

300 g/¾ lb mange tout, sliced lengthways

2 small courgettes, shredded lengthways

50 g/2 oz pimiento-stuffed olives, sliced

salt and freshly ground black pepper

2 tbsp chopped fresh parsley

2 tbsp chopped fresh mint

squeeze of fresh lime juice

fresh herbs and lime slices, to garnish

Bring a large saucepan of water to the boil and add the vermicelli with a dash of olive oil. Cook for about 5 minutes, stirring occasionally, until tender. Drain and set aside.

Melt the butter in a large frying pan and sauté the sliced mange tout and shredded courgette for about 5 minutes, stirring occasionally.

Add the remaining ingredients except the lime juice to the vegetable mixture and cook for a further 5 minutes, stirring occasionally. Mix in the vermicelli and cook for 2–3 minutes, until heated through. Squeeze the fresh lime juice over the mixture and serve garnished with fresh herbs and lime slices.

SPAGHETTINI WITH LEEKS AND ONIONS

Serves 4

Red onions have a much sweeter flavour than regular onions. Their colour complements the green of the leek.

INGREDIENTS

4 tbsp olive oil

1 large red onion, peeled and cut into wedges

2–3 young leeks, trimmed and sliced

4 shallots, peeled and cut into thin slivers

2 x 400 g/14 oz tins chopped tomatoes

◀ *Verde Vegetables with Vermicelli*

Heat the oil in a frying pan and gently sauté the onion for 5 minutes. Add the leeks and shallots and continue to sauté for 3 more minutes. Add the chopped tomatoes with seasoning to taste and simmer gently for 5–8 minutes or until the sauce has been reduced by about half.

Meanwhile, cook the spaghettini in plenty of salted boiling water for 1–2 minutes or until 'al dente'. Drain thoroughly and return to the pan. Add the sauce to the pan with the chopped parsley and toss lightly. Serve immediately, handing around the cheese separately.

PROVENÇAL GREEN BEANS WITH PASTA

Serves 4–6

A delicious way to serve green beans, piping hot with freshly grated Parmesan cheese.

INGREDIENTS

2 tbsp olive oil

3 garlic cloves, crushed

1 onion, chopped

3 tbsp chopped fresh thyme

450 g/1 lb green beans

400 g/14 oz tin chopped tomatoes

2 tbsp tomato paste

scant 450 ml/16 fl oz vegetable stock

180 ml/6½ fl oz dry red wine

salt and freshly ground black pepper

450 g/1 lb dried pasta

2 tbsp butter

freshly grated Parmesan cheese

Heat the oil in a large frying pan and sauté the garlic and onion for about 3 minutes, until softened. Add the thyme, beans, tomatoes, tomato paste, vegetable stock and wine, season with salt and freshly ground black pepper and stir well to combine. Cover and cook gently for 25–30 minutes until the beans are tender. Remove the lid and cook for a further 5–8 minutes, stirring occasionally, until the sauce has thickened slightly.

Meanwhile, bring a large saucepan of water to the boil and add the pasta with a dash of olive oil. Cook for about 10 minutes, stirring occasionally, until tender. Drain and return to the saucepan. Toss in butter and freshly ground black pepper.

Serve the beans with the hot, buttered pasta and freshly grated Parmesan cheese.

PASTA BASKETS WITH VEGETABLES

Serves 4

The special piece of equipment used in this recipe is known by the French as a *nid d'oiseau*,
which translated means a 'bird's nest'. It is a small metal basket in a basket on long handles, commonly used to make edible
baskets of potato, filo pastry and, in this case, vermicelli.

INGREDIENTS

100 g/4 oz dried vermicelli

dash of olive oil

vegetable oil, for deep-frying

FILLING

2 tbsp sesame oil

2 garlic cloves, crushed

16 baby corncobs

100 g/¼ lb mange tout

2 carrots, thinly sliced

3 tbsp soy sauce

1 tbsp toasted sesame seeds

Bring a large saucepan of water to the boil, and add the vermicelli with a dash of olive oil. Cook for about 5 minutes, stirring occasionally, until tender. Drain and set aside.

Heat the oil for deep frying, and pack the cooked vermicelli into the bird's nest, if using. Otherwise, fry the vermicelli in batches in a frying basket. Cook for 3–5 minutes in hot oil, until the vermicelli is crisp and golden. Remove the basket from the bird's nest, and drain on absorbent kitchen paper. Repeat the process to make three more baskets. Arrange the baskets of loose vermicelli on individual serving plates. Set aside.

To make the filling, heat the sesame oil in a frying pan and sauté the garlic for 1–2 minutes. Add the corn, mange tout and carrots, stir and cook for 3–5 minutes, until tender. Stir in the soy sauce and sprinkle with the sesame seeds. Cook for a further 2 minutes, then spoon into the vermicelli baskets or onto a bed of vermicelli to serve.

MINTY CRAB, PEAR AND PASTA SALAD

Serves 4

The dressing used in this recipe was found whilst looking through an old cookbook. It has been updated by using a flavoured vinegar and oil, and once you have tried it, this recipe will quickly become a firm favourite.

INGREDIENTS

225 g/8 oz cooked fresh pasta, such as tricolored spaghetti

200 g/7 oz white crab meat, flaked

2 oranges, peeled and cut into sections

2 pink grapefruit, peeled and cut into sections

2 tbsp chopped fresh mint

50 g/2 oz pecan halves

2 ripe pears

150 ml/¼ pint walnut oil

4 tbsp extra-virgin olive oil

1 tbsp orange or raspberry vinegar

salt and ground black pepper

Place the cooked pasta in a bowl and add the flaked crab meat, orange and grapefruit sections, chopped mint and pecan halves. Toss lightly and spoon into a serving bowl.

For the dressing, peel and core the pears, then place in a food processor. Gradually blend the pears with the walnut and then the olive oil. Add the orange or raspberry vinegar with seasoning and blend for 30 seconds or until smooth. Pour over the salad, toss lightly and serve.

FETTUCCINE WITH TOMATOES AND MOZZARELLA

Serves 4

This delicious summertime salad can be made well in advance and left to marinate for up to 3 hours.

INGREDIENTS

300 g/12 oz dried egg fettuccine

dash of olive oil

450 g/1 lb (about 2 medium) beefsteak tomatoes, skinned, seeded and sliced

5 tbsp extra virgin olive oil

2 garlic cloves, crushed

6 tbsp chopped fresh basil

2 tbsp chopped fresh oregano

100 g/¼ lb mozzarella cheese, cut into 1-cm/½-inch cubes

40 g/1½ oz freshly grated Romano or Parmesan cheese

salt and freshly ground black pepper

Bring a large saucepan of water to the boil and add the fettuccine with a dash of olive oil. Cook for about 10 minutes, stirring occasionally, until tender. Drain and rinse under cold running water. Drain again and set aside.

In a large bowl, combine the sliced tomato flesh with the remaining ingredients and toss together lightly. Add the cooked fettuccine, and mix lightly to coat in the oil. Serve this salad at room temperature with warm garlic bread.

Minty Crab, Pear and Pasta Salad ▶

HERBED TOMATO AND PASTA SALAD

Serves 4

Served with crusty bread, this makes a splendid starter or light lunch. It does, of course, rely on fresh basil for success.

INGREDIENTS

225 g/8 oz fresh pasta shapes

450 g/1 lb ripe tomatoes, peeled, seeded and quartered

6 spring onions, chopped

1 garlic clove, crushed

salt and freshly ground black pepper

4–6 tbsp olive oil

6 fresh basil sprigs

Cook the fresh pasta shapes in boiling salted water for 3 minutes, drain and set aside to cool. Mix the tomatoes with the spring onions. Add the garlic, seasoning and olive oil, and mix well. Cover and set aside to marinate for 1 hour.

Toss the tomato mixture into the pasta. Use scissors to shred the basil, with the soft stem ends, over the pasta. Mix well and serve at once.

Pasta and Baked Pepper Salad

Serves 4

Skinning peppers is a boring task but the transformation in flavour is worth the effort. You can use any combination of peppers for colour. This is another salad that makes a good first course; it is also an ideal accompaniment for barbecued meat or poultry. Instead of store-bought pasta shapes, you can use your own small pasta squares.

INGREDIENTS

225 g/8 oz fresh pasta shapes

2 red peppers

1 green pepper

1 yellow pepper

4 tbsp olive oil

2 tbsp chopped fresh parsley

1 tbsp lemon juice

salt and freshly ground black pepper

50 g/2 oz tin anchovy fillets, drained and chopped

2 eggs, hard-boiled and chopped

Cook the pasta in boiling salted water for 3 minutes and drain well. Transfer it to a shallow serving bowl.

Grill the peppers until they are scorched all over. This is fairly time-consuming, as you have to make sure that all the skin is blistered. After the skin has lifted away from the pepper flesh it can be peeled off easily, and any remains should be rubbed off under cold running water.

Dry the peppers on absorbent kitchen paper, halve them and cut out all their seeds and core. Slice the peppers across into thin strips and scatter them over the pasta. Mix the olive oil, parsley and lemon juice with seasoning to taste. Stir in the anchovies, then use a spoon to trickle this dressing evenly over the peppers and pasta. Sprinkle the chopped hard-boiled egg over the pasta and serve.

MIXED PASTA SALAD

Serves 4

A good one for all those parties and picnics!

INGREDIENTS

225 g/8 oz pasta shapes

125 g/5 oz frozen corn

125 g/5 oz frozen peas

1 carrot, diced

4 celery stalks, diced

1 green pepper, seeded and diced

6 spring onions, chopped

2 tbsp chopped fresh parsley

225 g/8 oz mayonnaise

3 tbsp single cream

225 g/8 oz garlic sausage, roughly chopped

salt and freshly ground black pepper

Cook the pasta in boiling salted water for 3 minutes, drain well, then place the pasta in a bowl. Place the corn, peas and carrot in a saucepan and add water to cover.

Bring to the boil, add the diced celery and bring back to the boil, then cook for a further 5 minutes. Drain the vegetables and add them to the pasta. Allow to cool.

Mix in the green pepper, spring onions, and parsley. Thin the mayonnaise with the cream, then toss this dressing into the salad. Lastly, lightly mix in the chopped garlic sausage and taste for seasoning.

RUOTI WITH SALAMI

Serves 4

A delicious pasta platter for hot summer days.

INGREDIENTS

2 celery stalks

1 dessert apple, peeled

juice of 1 lemon

225 g/8 oz cooked ruoti wheels

125 g/5 oz mayonnaise

1 small lettuce

8 slices of salami

2 tomatoes and celery leaves, to garnish

Remove the strings from the celery with a sharp knife and cut into thin slices. Dice the dessert apple and mix with the celery. Sprinkle the lemon juice on the celery and apple, and arrange on the bottom of a dish lined with lettuce.

Mix the pasta with the mayonnaise, and arrange on top of the apples and celery. Roll up slices of salami and arrange in a wheel pattern on the pasta wheels. Garnish with tomato wedges and some celery leaves in the centre.

Mixed Pasta Salad ▶

TAGLIARINI WITH GREEN BEANS AND GARLIC

Serves 4–6

A delicious summer salad, hot main course or vegetable accompaniment, this dish is suitable for almost any occasion.

INGREDIENTS

300 g/12 oz dried tagliarini

dash of olive oil, plus 4 tbsp

300 g/¾ lb green beans

1 medium potato, cut into 1-cm/½-inch cubes

3 garlic cloves, chopped

5 tbsp chopped fresh sage

salt and freshly ground black pepper

freshly grated Parmesan cheese, to serve

Bring a large saucepan of water to the boil, and add the tagliarini with a dash of olive oil. Cook for about 10 minutes, stirring occasionally, until tender. Drain and set aside.

Cook the beans and potato cubes in a large saucepan of boiling water for about 10 minutes, until tender. Drain well, and set aside to keep warm.

Heat the remaining olive oil in a large frying pan, add the garlic and sage, and season with salt and freshly ground black pepper. Sauté for 2–3 minutes, then add the cooked beans and potato. Cook for 1–2 minutes, then add the cooked tagliarini, and mix well.

Cook for about 5 minutes, stirring occasionally, then transfer to a warmed serving dish. Sprinkle with freshly grated Parmesan cheese and serve.

Wholefood Pasta Salad

Serves 4

The natural yoghurt dressing makes this salad ideal for those who are watching their weight.

INGREDIENTS

225 g/8 oz whole-wheat fusilli
125 g/5 oz plain yoghurt
½ tsp cumin
½ garlic clove, crushed
salt and freshly ground black pepper
juice of 1 lemon
1 small lettuce
1 bunch watercress
1 tbsp bran

Cook the fusilli for 10–12 minutes, drain and rinse in cold water. Allow to drain well in a colander. Put the yoghurt into a bowl and mix with the cumin, garlic and seasoning. Add a few drops of lemon juice.

Toss the pasta in the yoghurt dressing. Arrange the lettuce and watercress in a salad bowl, and sprinkle with lemon juice. Arrange the pasta in the centre of the bowl and sprinkle with the bran. Cucumber and tomatoes can be added.

CHICKEN AVOCADO PASTA SALAD

Serves 4

Any wholewheat pasta shape, including shells, fusilli or short cut macaroni, may be used for this recipe.
Leave the avocados in lemon juice until just before serving so that they do not discolour.

INGREDIENTS

225 g/8 oz pasta, cooked

6 spring onions, finely chopped

125 g/5 oz mayonnaise

2 ripe avocados

250 g/10 oz cooked chicken, chopped

salt and freshly ground black pepper

1 tsp lemon juice

2 tomatoes, skinned and sliced

1 red pepper, seeded and blanched

parsley or watercress (optional)

Place the cooked pasta in a bowl. Add the spring onions to the pasta with the mayonnaise.

Remove the skins from the avocados, cut in half, and remove the seeds. Cut eight thin slices for garnish and chop the remainder. Add to the pasta and mayonnaise mixture with the cooked chicken. Season well and add a few drops of lemon juice. Place the sliced avocado in the remaining lemon juice.

Arrange the salad in a bowl which has been lined with the tomato slices. Garnish with slices of blanched pepper and the sliced avocados. Arrange parsley or watercress around the dish. If preparing in advance, leave the avocados in lemon juice until just before serving.

MINTY PEPPER SALAD

Serves 4

Serve this cool, light and refreshing salad for a summer lunch, or make it for a picnic since it packs and travels well.

INGREDIENTS

750 g/1 lb 12 oz dried macaroni

dash of olive oil, plus extra for drizzling

1 yellow pepper, seeded and cut into 1-cm/½-inch diamonds

1 green pepper, seeded and cut into 1-cm/½-inch diamonds

400 g/14 oz tin artichoke hearts, drained and quartered

15 cm/6-inch piece of cucumber, sliced

handful of mint leaves

salt and freshly ground black pepper

125 g/5 oz freshly grated Parmesan cheese

Bring a large saucepan of water to the boil and add the macaroni with a dash of olive oil. Cook for about 10 minutes, stirring occasionally, until tender. Drain and rinse under cold running water. Drain again, then place in a large mixing bowl.

Add the remaining ingredients to the pasta and mix well to combine. Drizzle some olive oil over the salad, then serve.

Fusilli with Grapes and Goat's Cheese

Serves 4

This is delicious for a light lunch or as a starter. Serve with slices of French bread.

INGREDIENTS

2 slices round goat's cheese, each cut in 8 small wedges

150 g/6 oz seedless green grapes

2 bunches of watercress, trimmed and roughly shredded

4 spring onions, chopped

zest and juice of 1 orange

4 tbsp olive oil

salt and freshly ground black pepper

300 g/12 oz fresh fusilli

Mix the cheese, grapes, watercress and spring onions in a large bowl. Pour in the orange zest and juice and olive oil, then add a little salt and plenty of freshly ground black pepper. Mix well. Divide the hot, freshly drained pasta between four serving plates, then top each with a quarter of the cheese mixture. Serve at once.

Desserts and Puddings

BAKED PASTA PUDDING

Serves 4

This unsophisticated dessert will probably become a firm favourite with the adults as well as children.

INGREDIENTS

100 g/4 oz dried tagliatelle

dash of sunflower oil

50 g/2 oz butter

2 eggs

100 g/4 oz sugar

pinch of cinnamon

grated peel of 1 lemon

few drops of vanilla essence

4 tbsp seedless raisins

sieved icing sugar, to decorate

Pre-heat the oven to 190°C/ 375°F/Gas Mark 5. Bring a large saucepan of water to the boil and add the tagliatelle with a dash of sunflower oil. Cook for about 10 minutes, stirring occasionally, until tender. Drain and rinse under cold running water. Drain again and set aside.

Place the butter in a shallow, oven-proof dish, and melt in the oven for about 5 minutes. Remove from the oven and carefully swirl the melted butter around the sides of the dish. Set aside to cool slightly.

In a mixing bowl, whisk together the eggs and sugar until thick and frothy. Whisk in the cinnamon, lemon peel, vanilla essence and reserved melted butter. Stir in the seedless raisins and cooked tagliatelle until evenly coated in the egg mixture.

Transfer the pudding mixture to the prepared dish, and distribute evenly. Bake for about 35–40 minutes, until the mixture has set and is crisp and golden. Allow to cool slightly. Serve warm, decorated with sieved icing sugar.

FRUIT DREAMS

Serves 6

This dessert can be made using plain pasta, or really indulge and use chocolate pasta instead.

INGREDIENTS

½ quantity plain Pasta Dough (page 27)

225 g/8 oz strawberries, sliced

6 tbsp maple syrup

225 g/8 oz raspberries

300 ml/½ pint whipped cream

2–3 tbsp toasted chopped hazelnuts

Make the pasta dough, roll it into a 30-cm/12-inch square and cut it into 2.5 cm/1-inch strips. Cut the strips at an angle to make diamond shapes (rather like cutting almond paste leaves when decorating a cake). Cook the pasta in boiling water for 3 minutes and drain.

In a bowl, mix the strawberries with the maple syrup. Add the drained pasta and mix lightly. Mix the raspberries with the pasta and strawberries, taking care to keep them whole. Divide the fruit and pasta between 6 dishes. Top with generous swirls of cream, then sprinkle with toasted chopped hazelnuts. Serve at once.

Baked Pasta Pudding ▶

Honey, Orange and Almond Tagliatelle

Serves 4–6

Here's a really quick and easy dessert. Pasta tossed in butter and honey syrup makes a perfect pasta dish to end a meal.

INGREDIENTS

225 g/8 oz dried egg tagliatelle

dash of sunflower oil

4 oranges

5 tbsp clear honey

3 tbsp soft light brown sugar

1 tbsp lemon juice

3 tbsp butter

40 g/1½ oz flaked almonds

Bring a large saucepan of water to the boil and add the tagliatelle with a dash of sunflower oil. Cook for about 8–10 minutes, stirring occasionally, until tender. Drain and set aside.

Whilst the pasta is cooking, peel and slice three of the oranges and cut the slices in half. Squeeze the juice from the remaining orange into a small saucepan. Add the honey, sugar and lemon juice. Bring to the boil, stirring to dissolve the sugar, and simmer for 1–2 minutes, until syrupy.

Melt the butter in a large frying pan and fry the slivered almonds until golden. Stir in the freshly cooked tagliatelle-and-honey syrup, heat through, then quickly stir in the orange slices. Serve immediately.

WINTER FRUIT COMPOTE WITH TINY PASTA SHAPES

Serves 4–6

Try this for breakfast. It needs to be started the day before, and will keep for several days in the refrigerator. Make up your own selection of mixed dried fruit, if you prefer.

INGREDIENTS

about 15 dried apricots

125 g/5 oz dried apple rings or chunks

about 12 dried pears

8 dried figs

25 g/1 oz dried cherries

4 cloves

2 allspice berries

1 cinnamon stick

finely grated peel and juice of 1 orange

300 ml/½ pint weak tea

150 ml/5 fl oz water

3 tbsp soft brown sugar

4 tbsp dried pastina

Place the dried fruit in a bowl with the spices, orange peel and juice, tea, and water. Cover, and leave to soak overnight.

The next day, spoon the fruit compote into a saucepan, bring to a boil, and simmer for 15 minutes, adding a little more water if necessary. Stir in the soft brown sugar and dried pastina, and cook for a further 8–10 minutes, until the pastina is tender. Serve warm or cold.

CHOCOLATE PASTA TORTE

Serves 8

A decadently rich dessert to serve on special occasions. Use good-quality semi-sweet dessert chocolate – ordinary cooking chocolate just won't taste the same.

INGREDIENTS

100 g/4 oz dried vermicelli

dash of sunflower oil, plus extra for greasing

300 g/12 oz semisweet chocolate, broken into pieces

4 tbsp water

100 g/4 oz unsalted butter

100 g/4 oz sugar

zest of 1 orange

225 g/8 oz tin unsweetened chestnut purée

4 tbsp brandy

40 g/1½ oz ground almonds

50 g/2 oz flaked almonds

5 tbsp double cream

chocolate leaves, to decorate

Bring a large saucepan of water to the boil and add the vermicelll with a dash of sunflower oil. Cook for about 6 minutes, stirring occasionally, until tender. Drain and rinse under cold running water. Drain again, and set aside.

Lightly oil a 17.5-cm/7-inch round springform or loose-bottomed cake pan and line with greaseproof paper. Lightly oil the paper.

Place 225 g/8 oz of the chocolate and the water in a small saucepan, and heat gently until melted. Set aside to cool.

Meanwhile, cream together the butter, sugar, and orange zest until light and fluffy, then gradually beat in the chestnut purée. Add the melted chocolate to the brandy and mix well. Stir in the flaked almonds and freshly cooked vermicelli. Turn the mixture into the prepared pan and smooth over the surface. Refrigerate overnight.

Put the remaining chocolate and the cream into a small bowl over a saucepan of simmering water and heat gently, stirring occasionally, until melted and smooth. Remove the bowl from the heat.

Remove the torte from the pan, and place on a wire cooling rack. Pour the melted chocolate mixture evenly over the cake, using a spatula to coat the sides. Leave to set.

Carefully transfer the torte to a serving plate and decorate with chocolate leaves.

FRUIT RAVIOLI WITH A RED COULIS

Serves 6–8

Look out for dried mango and pineapple in health food stores and delicatessens. Alternatively, use a mixture of chopped candied fruits in this recipe.

INGREDIENTS

FILLING

about 15 ready-to-eat dried apricots, finely chopped

125 g/5 oz dried mango or pineapple, finely chopped

zest of 1 orange

½ tsp cinnamon

2 tbsp amaretto liqueur (optional)

⅔ quantity Pasta Dough (page 27), omitting the salt, using 1 tbsp fresh orange juice instead of the water and adding the zest of 1 orange to the eggs

lightly beaten egg

dash of sunflower oil

COULIS

250 g/10 oz fresh raspberries

100 g/4 oz icing sugar, sifted

TO DECORATE

finely chopped pistachio nuts

fresh raspberries

mint sprigs

First make the filling: mix together the apricots, dried mango or pineapple, orange zest and cinnamon. Add the amaretto, if desired.

To make the ravioli, cut the pasta dough in half, and roll out one half to a 35 × 25 cm/14 × 10-inch rectangle. Trim the edges of the dough and cover with cling film to prevent it from drying.

Roll out the other piece of pasta dough to the same size. Place half teaspoonfuls of the filling mixture in lines 2 cm/¾ inch apart on one piece of dough. Lightly brush beaten egg between the filling mixture and carefully lay the second piece of dough over the top. Starting at one end, press the dough down around the filling, carefully pushing out any trapped air. Using a sharp knife, pastry wheel or round cutter, cut in lines between the filling to divide the ravioli into squares.

Cook the ravioli in a large saucepan of boiling water with a dash of sunflower oil for about 5 minutes, stirring occasionally, until tender. Drain and set aside to cool slightly.

Meanwhile, make the coulis: place the raspberries and icing sugar in a food processor or blender, and purée until smooth. Sieve to remove the seeds.

Serve the ravioli on individual plates with the coulis, and decorate with chopped pistachio nuts, fresh raspberries and mint sprigs.

CINNAMON FETTUCCINE WITH APPLE AND CINNAMON SAUCE

Serves 6

This delightful autumn dessert is delicious served with cream. Ground mixed spice makes a good alternative to cinnamon.

INGREDIENTS

⅔ quantity Pasta Dough (page 27), (omitting the salt and adding 2 tsp ground cinnamon to the flour)

SAUCE

3–4 medium dessert apples, peeled, cored, and sliced

zest of 1 lemon

¼ tsp ground cinnamon

3 tbsp water, plus 180 ml/6½ fl oz

3 tbsp soft light-brown sugar

65 g/2½ oz seedless raisins

1 tbsp butter, plus a little extra

2 tsp arrowroot blended with 2 tsp cold water

flour, to dredge

dash of sunflower oil

Keep the pasta dough wrapped in cling film to prevent it from drying out, and set aside.

To make the sauce, put the apples into a saucepan with the lemon zest, cinnamon and 3 tablespoons water. Cover and cook gently until the apples have softened. Remove about half of the apple slices from the saucepan, and set aside. Place the remaining apples in a food processor or blender, and purée until smooth.

Return the purée to the saucepan and stir in the reserved apples, sugar, seedless raisins, 1 tablespoon butter, arrowroot mixture and 180 ml/⅔ cup water. Cook for about 5 minutes, stirring constantly, until bubbling and thickened. Set aside.

To make the fettuccine, roll out the pasta dough very thinly on a floured surface. Lightly dredge with flour, then roll up and use a sharp knife to cut the dough into 5-mm/¼-inch wide slices. Shake out the noodles as they are cut, and pile them on a floured baking tray.

To cook the fettuccine, bring a large saucepan of water to the boil and add the pasta with a dash of sunflower oil. Cook for about 3 minutes, stirring occasionally, until tender.

CHOCOLATE PASTA WITH CHOCOLATE SAUCE

Serves 6

A chocoholic's dream – it has to be tasted to be believed!

INGREDIENTS

⅔ quantity Pasta Dough (page 27), omitting the salt and adding 25 g/1 oz unsweetened cocoa and 3 tbsp icing sugar to the flour

dash of sunflower oil

SAUCE

150 g/6 oz semi-sweet chocolate, broken into pieces

180 ml/6½ fl oz milk

2 tbsp golden syrup

2 tbsp butter

TO DECORATE

fresh strawberries

amaretti cookies

Keep the pasta dough wrapped in cling film to prevent it drying out, and set aside.

To make the sauce, place all the ingredients in a small saucepan and heat gently, stirring, for about 5 minutes, until melted, smooth and shiny. Cool slightly.

Roll out the pasta dough thinly on a floured surface and cut into rounds with a 5-cm/2-inch round plain or fluted cutter. Pinch the sides of each dough round together, pleating in the middle. Set the bows aside on baking sheets lined with greaseproof paper.

Bring a large saucepan of water to the boil, and add the pasta with a dash of sunflower oil. Cook for about 3 minutes, stirring occasionally, until tender. Drain and return to the saucepan.

Pour the chocolate sauce over the pasta and stir gently to coat. Serve decorated with fresh strawberries and amaretti cookies.

PLUM AND BLACKBERRY COMPOTE

Serves 6

A good sauce for serving with plain home-made pasta in the autumn. Remember that dessert pasta looks more attractive
if it is stamped out in pretty shapes using aspic cutters.

INGREDIENTS

100 g/4 oz granulated sugar

zest and juice of 1 orange

180 ml/6½ fl oz dry cider

1 cinnamon stick

2 cloves

450 g/1 lb plums, halved and pitted

450 g/1 lb blackberries

Place the sugar, orange zest and juice, cider, cinnamon and cloves in a large saucepan. Heat gently, stirring, until the sugar melts. Allow the syrup to infuse over very low heat for 15 minutes, then bring it to simmering point and add the plums

Poach the plums gently for 3 minutes, then add the blackberries and cook for 2 minutes. (Do not overcook the fruit until it becomes soft; the cooking time for the plums varies according to their texture). Ladle this fruit sauce over freshly cooked, drained pasta, removing the spices as you do so.

RUM AND RAISIN SHAPES

Serves 6

A rich and fruity dessert to complete a special meal.

INGREDIENTS

65 g/2½ oz chopped raisins

1½ tbsp finely chopped candied peel

ground almonds

2 tbsp icing sugar

8 tbsp rum

⅔ quantity Pasta Dough (page 27)

1 egg, beaten

100 g/4 oz crab apple jelly

4 tbsp unsweetened apple juice

2 tbsp finely chopped candied orange peel, to decorate

thick yoghurt or cream, to serve

Mix the raisins, candied peel, ground almonds and icing sugar. Stir in enough of the rum to bind the ingredients together; the rest of the rum is required for the glaze.

Cut the dough in half and roll out one portion into a 30 cm/12 inch square. Use a 5-cm/2-inch round fluted cutter or a shaped cutter to stamp out pieces of dough. If you work neatly, you will get 36 shapes.

Brush a piece of dough with the beaten egg, place a little of the rum and raisin mixture in the middle, then cover with a second piece of dough. Pinch the edges together firmly to seal in the filling. Continue until all the shapes are used, then repeat with the second portion of dough. Place the finished rounds on a plate lightly dusted with cornflour and keep them loosely covered to prevent them drying whilst you fill the other shapes.

When all the pasta is filled, cook in boiling water for 5 minutes and drain well. To make the glaze, gently heat the crab apple jelly with the apple juice until the jelly melts. Bring to the boil, then remove from the heat and stir in the remaining rum.

Serve the freshly cooked pasta coated with the apple glaze. To decorate, sprinkle with the chopped candied orange peel and offer yoghurt or thick cream.

INDEX